BASICS

GLASS CONSTRUCTION

\\ANDREAS ACHILLES \\DIANE NAVRATIL

BASICS

GLASS CONSTRUCTION

BIRKHÄUSER
BASEL · BOSTON · BERLIN

CONTENTS

FOREWORD

Glass is one of the most attractive building materials. It connects spaces to one another while separating them. The various types of glass range from complete transparency and openness to reflective glass that provides hermetic separation for facades. This diversity makes glass unique in architectural design.

Glass in its pure form is a material that needs to be carefully considered. It breaks very quickly and often unexpectedly and is sensitive to mechanical stress. Thanks to advances in research, however, no other building material offers such great potential for development or such a multifaceted spectrum of possible uses—including bulletproof glass and the creation of bearing structures entirely of glass.

The use of glass as a building material is always coupled with knowledge of technical properties and possibilities. Only by knowing the properties of various glasses, the components and elements of a glass construction, and the limits of the material can an architect develop creative solutions using this material and transcend the existing limits again and again.

The present volume, *Glass Construction*, is part of a subset of the series on construction. It begins by considering construction and conveys to the reader an understanding of the specific properties of glass and the possibilities that it offers as a building material. By increasing knowledge of the building material and revealing complex structures and applications, it enables students of architecture to consider their own creative solutions beyond the standardized offerings of the construction industry. Many advances in glass construction have resulted not only from laboratory research on the material but also from innovative and unconventional designs by architects who have met the challenges and provided stimuli for ever new developments and uses. *Basics Glass Construction* is intended to inspire students to use their knowledge of glass to explore the possibilities for their own designs and perhaps even develop new approaches.

Bert Bielefeld, Editor

INTRODUCTION

Like few other materials, glass possesses a symbolism that transcends mere function and exerts a particular fascination. The glass windows of the Gothic period already deliberately played with light in order to produce a feeling of transcendence. In the architectural visions of modernism, this transparent material took on central significance, although glass played different roles, depending on the theoretical approach in question. Glass was appreciated not only for its transparency, which permitted an almost dematerialized shell and hence flowing, open spaces, but also for its graceful, angular, and glittering qualities. The emancipation of glass from its role as a filler in relatively small windows to become an autonomous element would prove particularly forward-looking. Problems in terms of energy conservation and disregard of the physical requirements of construction put a temporary end to the euphoria over this material.

Today, thanks, among other things, to a turn to solutions that make sense for energy conservation, and the development of glass that provides effective insulation and solar control, glass has once again become a high-performance material. As such, it fulfills both functional and design requirements and opens up ever new areas of application.

For all the possibilities that glass offers, however, it should not be forgotten that it is a very brittle material. Glass breaks suddenly and without warning when it is overstressed in particular places. That calls for precise knowledge of the nature of the material and great care in planning and implementing glass structures.

This book introduces students step by step to the basics of glass as a building material and to glass construction. In the first three chapters, the reader learns the properties and diversity of today's types of glass, then the most important principles for constructing with it, and finally the different areas of application and their constraints. The technical fundamentals are explained intelligibly and in a structured way in terms of their principles and by means of simple examples. In this way, students obtain an overview of the current state of technology and are in a position to plan their own projects using glass as a building material and to make their own ideas reality.

GLASS AS A BUILDING MATERIAL

THE PRODUCTION OF GLASS

Composition
Glass is produced by heating a mixture that consists largely of silica (silicon dioxide) and soda ash (sodium carbonate). Soda ash serves as a so-called flux to reduce the high melting point of silica (approx. 1700 °C). The melting that then takes place above 1100 °C is amorphous—that is, virtually no crystals are formed. Because the structure of glass resembles that of fluids, glass is sometimes called a "supercooled liquid." › Tab. 1

Types of glass
The most commonly used glass in architecture is soda-lime glass, the main components of which are silicon dioxide, calcium oxide, and sodium oxide. Borosilicate glass, which contains boron oxide rather than calcium oxide, is often used as fire-resistant glass thanks to its high chemical and thermal stability. Lead glass, which is produced from lead crystal, among other things, and special glass, which is used in optical devices, for example, have no significance for architecture. Glass ceramic, by contrast, has recently begun to be used to clad facades. Transparent synthetic glass such as acrylic glass and polycarbonate is lighter and easier to work than mineral glass, but because it has a lower surface hardness it is considerably more sensitive to scratching and thus not as durable.

BASIC PRODUCTS

Glass products that are formed during production in a "hot" state or immediately after cooling are generally referred to as basic products or basic glass. Various kinds of basic glass are employed in architecture. In addition to clear flat glasses with a smooth surface, glasses with specially designed surfaces or special shapes are also used. Basic glass is often further processed or finished. › Chapter Processing and finishing

Tab.1: Composition of glass according to EN 572, Part 1		
Silicon dioxide	SiO_2	69-74%
Calcium oxide	CaO	5-12%
Sodium oxide	Na_2O	12-16%
Magnesium oxide	MgO	0-6%
Aluminum oxide	Al_2O_3	0-3%

We describe below the types of basic glass relevant to architecture and how they are produced.

Float glass

Float method

Float glass is the most commonly used form of basic glass. Its name derives from the process by which it is produced. The float method developed in 1960 was a milestone in the history of the production of flat glass, because it became possible for the first time to produce large quantities of clear, transparent glass with nearly flat surfaces.

Production begins by melting the raw materials, referred to as "batch," in a furnace. Next, the molten glass runs onto a flat bath of molten tin. Because it has a lower specific gravity, the glass floats on the tin, which gives it its flat surface. This produces an endless glass ribbon that slowly hardens; its thickness is determined by the speed with which it is pulled over the tin bath. After passing through this tin bath, or "float bath," the glass ribbon passes through a cooling zone, and finally is cut into plates. › Fig. 1

The standard format, known as <u>ribbon size</u>, is 600 × 321 cm. Its standard or <u>nominal thicknesses</u> are 2, 3, 4, 5, 6, 8, 10, 12, 15, and 19 mm.

Sheet or window glass

The term "window glass" is somewhat misleading, since float glass is usually used for windows these days. Sheet or window glass is now produced only individually in <u>drawn glass facilities</u>, in which the glass ribbon is drawn horizontally or even vertically from the furnace. Today this process is used to produce particular kinds of colored glass, or for special

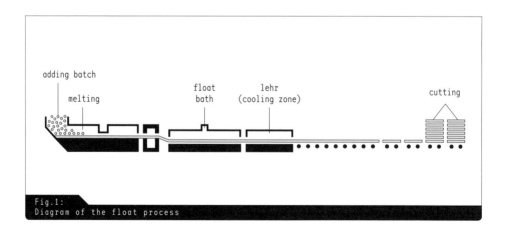

adding batch
melting
float bath
lehr (cooling zone)
cutting

Fig.1:
Diagram of the float process

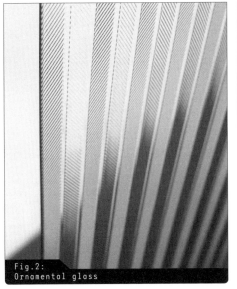

Fig.2:
Ornamental glass

Fig.3:
Various types of profile glass

glass such as very thin glass. The surface quality is somewhat poorer than that of float glass, as waves (called striae) are visible.

Cast glass

Rolling method
Cast or rolled glass is produced using the rolling method, in which the glass mass is formed into an endless ribbon between two water-cooled rollers. Decorations engraved into the rollers give the glass ribbon a surface structure. In order to produce wired glass or ornamental wired glass, a wire net can be rolled into the glass. Cast glass is also called ornamental glass because of its structure or ornamental surface, and its uses include partitions and facade openings where an open view through is neither desired nor required. › Chapter Design glass, Ornamental glass

Profile glass

Profile glass is produced using a process similar to that for cast glass. In addition to a surface structure, the glass is given a cross section (U-profile) that is structurally advantageous, so that considerable spans become possible. › Fig. 3

Because it is economical, profile glass has been and continues to be used for the facades of industrial buildings. Nowadays, profile glass is also a very popular building material in architecture generally. › Chapter Applications, Profile glass

Fig.4:
Glass bricks

Pressed glass

Pressed glass is the general term for glass bricks, glass ceiling tiles, and concrete glass. These are made by fusing two bodies of glass pressed in forms (pressing method). When cooled, the air in the hollow space within the glass brick is under low pressure, which makes it nearly impossible for condensation to form. Glass bricks are often used in interiors or as translucent elements in solid exterior walls. Architectural glass is used primarily in ferroconcrete construction, since it is also well suited to higher structural loads. › Fig. 4

PROCESSING AND FINISHING

Most types of basic glass are further processed and finished after manufacture, which offers an opportunity to influence not only its form and shape but also the physical and structural properties. The spectrum of finishing processes ranges from mechanical and heat treatments to coating and designing the surfaces.

Mechanical processing

Processing such as cutting, boring, grinding, and polishing are generally labeled mechanical processing or mechanical finishing.

Cutting

Glass is <u>cut</u> into its desired shape. It is not really a cutting process, since the cutting wheel or diamond merely scratches the glass surface, and then the glass is broken by gently bending it along the scratched line. The glass coming directly from the floating machine is cut to ribbon size (600 × 321 cm) and is then given its desired final size in the finishing process. Cutting down and further processing are usually done by machine. For example, complex forms can be produced very precisely using a <u>water jet cutter</u>. The cutting is done with the aid of high-pressure jet of water (with

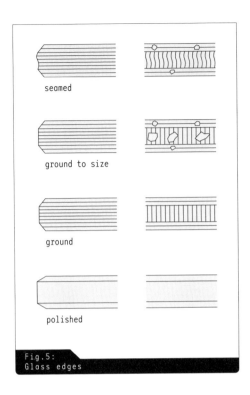

seamed

ground to size

ground

polished

Fig.5:
Glass edges

a water pressure up to 6000 bar) to which a cutting agent (an abrasive) is added.

Because the <u>edges</u> of the glass are still sharp after cutting, it is necessary to <u>treat the edges</u> both to prevent injury and for reasons relating to the production process. The treatments are distinguished in the following illustration and table. › Fig. 5 and Tab. 2

\\ Note:

The edge treatment affects not only the optical qualities of the glass plate but also its stability. Inhomogeneous or sharp edges increase the likelihood of damage to the glass (cracks, shells). The type of edge treatment must therefore be determined before awarding the contract; in some cases the pattern should as well.

Tab.2:
Edge treatments

Term	Definition
Cut	Untreated edge of glass with sharp perimeters as a result of cutting flat glass
Seamed	Cut edge with perimeters that have been smoothed with a grinding tool
Ground to size	Pane ground to the desired size. The edge may have shiny spots and shells.
Ground	The entire edge is ground to a semimatte finish. Shiny spots and shells are not permitted.
Polished	Ground edge is polished

Boring

Various applications in modern glass construction call for boreholes within the pane of glass. These boreholes make it possible to fasten the plates of glass at these points. Because glass is a very hard and brittle material, any mechanical processing must be done with an appropriate tool—boring, for example, should be done with a diamond-tip, water-cooled hollow drill. It should be drilled from both sides at once to prevent breaking through the opposite side. Because local tensions can be very high around the inner face of the hole, the panes are tempered after drilling to increase the strength of the glass.

Tempering

Bent

Bent or curved glass is produced from flat glass that is heated to approx. 600 °C to soften it and then brought into the desired form. Glass can be bent along one axis (cylindrically) or two (spherically), as for an all-glass domed ceiling, for example.

Tempering

Tempered safety glass (TSG) is tempered glass that has been heated to approx. 600 °C under controlled conditions in a tempering furnace and then cooled very quickly. The state of tension in the glass that this process produces can be "frozen," which considerably increases the bending strength of the material. › Fig. 6

In addition, TSG has a much higher thermal shock resistance than float glass. TSG can resist a thermal shock of as much as 150 K, whereas float glass can only withstand thermal shock of 40 K. TSG is considered safety glass, however, primarily due to the way it breaks. Because it is in

14

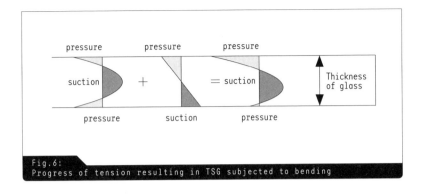

Fig.6:
Progress of tension resulting in TSG subjected to bending

state of internal tension, when it breaks it shatters suddenly into small fragments with blunt edges, which considerably reduces the risk of severe injury. On the one hand, because the fragments remain hooked together, it has the advantage that the broken pane usually stays in the frame. On the other, the hooked fragments also pose a threat to people underneath the glazing, as relatively large continuous pieces can fall down.

A rare but nonetheless undesirable property of toughened glass is spontaneous breakage: tiny inclusions of nickel sulfide, invisible to the naked eye, expand in volume over time, and can cause the pane to break unexpectedly even years after installation. One reliable means of detecting nickel sulfide inclusions is the heat soak test, in which the panes are warmed to about 290 °C. During a soak time of about four hours in the heat soak oven, the TSG panes with nickel sulfide inclusion will probably break and hence never be installed in the first place. In accordance with EN 14179, heat-soaked TSG is given the standard label TSG-H.

> ◧
Test heat soak

◧
\\ Note:
Because TSG is itself under tension, it cannot be cut, bored, or ground subsequently, as the pane would break. All the necessary steps for the mechanical finishing must therefore be completed before it is tempered.

15

Under certain daylight conditions and under polarized light, <u>anisotropies</u> become visible in TSG that has developed a directional (anisotropic) structure in the tempering process. Caused by double refraction of light rays in the areas of tension, they reveal patterns or clouds of structure in the spectral colors.

Heat-strength-
ened glass

<u>Heat-strengthened glass (HSG)</u> is produced by a process similar to that for TSG. It is, however, cooled more slowly, which reduces the pressure on the surface, which results in both lower bending strength and a different fracture pattern than that of TSG. The fracture pattern of HSG resembles that of untempered glass: a few radial cracks extend from the center of the fracture, and accordingly the fragments are large. Because the risk of serious injuries from cuts is larger than with TSG, HSG may not be rated safety glass.

Unlike TSG, HSG is not subject to spontaneous breakage from inclusions of nickel sulfide crystals. In exceptional cases, it is possible to treat (grind) the edges of HSG, but normally this should be done before tempering.

› ◍

Chemical processing

Compressive stress on the surface of glass can be produced chemically by dipping the glass into an electrolytic fluid. This process can even be used to temper very thin glass with spatially complex geometry. <u>Chemically tempered glass</u> has, however, only very minor significance in architecture.

Laminated glass and laminated safety glass

<u>Laminated safety glass (LSG)</u> is composed of at least two panes held together by a polyvinyl butyral (PVB) film. › Figs. 7 and 8

Such glass is often used in architecture, for overhead glass or other glass that prevents people from falling, and in the automotive industry. One essential reason for its use in such applications is that LSG holds

◍

\\ Note:
Note: The bending strength of HSG is 70 N/mm², that of TSG 120 N/mm² and that of normal glass 40 N/mm². Thermal shock resistance is 40 K for normal glass, 100 K for HSG, and 150 K for TSG. The following rule of thumb is used to estimate resistance to shock, pressure, and temperature: Factor 1 for normal glass, Factor 2 for HSG, and Factor 3 for TSG.

16

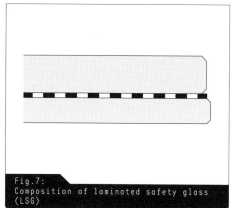

Fig.7:
Composition of laminated safety glass
(LSG)

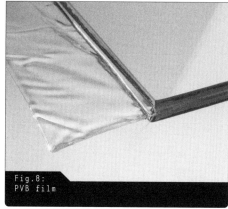

Fig.8:
PVB film

splinters together. When the pane breaks, the splinters of glass generally remain stuck to the transparent PVB film. It is difficult to pierce the film, which considerably reduces the risk of injury.

The viscoelastic PVB film is characterized by good adherence to glass, high tear strength, and high transparency and resistance to light. The nominal thickness of PVB film is 0.38 mm but it can be made many times that thickness if requested. Hence nominal thickness of 0.38 mm, 0.76 mm, and 1.52 mm are available. LSG is produced in three steps. First, a preliminary lamination between the glass and the film is produced in a clean room. Then the glass and film pass through the preliminary laminating oven in which the temperature and the pressure of the rollers increase the adherence of the glass and the film. The final laminate is created in an autoclave under high pressure and intense heat. Only then does the previously cloudy film obtain its high transparency.

Multilayer glass with interlayers made of materials other than PVB is generally referred to as <u>laminated glass</u>. Such glass does not usually meet the requirements for safety glass, and hence they may not be identified as such without special proof. Photovoltaic modules can be integrated into laminated glass, in which case ethylene-vinyl acetate (EVA) film is used.

Multilayer insulating glass

To improve heat insulation of the windows of buildings, insulating glass is now used almost exclusively. The linear lamination of two or more sheets of glass along the edge is called multilayer insulating glass (MIG). Dehumidified air or inert gas is hermetically sealed in the air space between the pane.

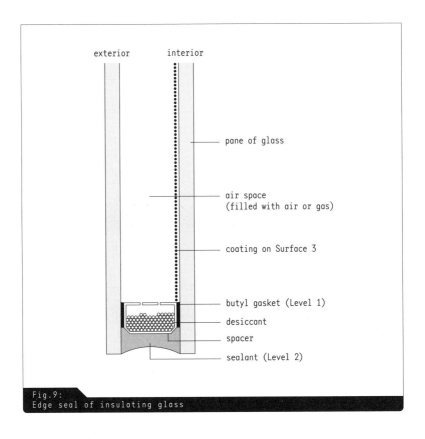

exterior   interior

— pane of glass

— air space
  (filled with air or gas)

— coating on Surface 3

— butyl gasket (Level 1)
— desiccant
— spacer
— sealant (Level 2)

Fig. 9:
Edge seal of insulating glass

Edge seal The <u>edge seal</u> running around the pane consists of a spacer of aluminum, stainless steel, or plastic and sealants. › Fig. 9

The spacer is filled with a hygroscopic dehumidifier that absorbs the residual humidity in the gas or air. This helps keep condensation from forming in the air space. The seal is provided by two levels of sealant. The first level consists of a butyl sealant that also glues the spacer to the glass; the second level consists of a permanently elastic sealant such as polysulfide, polyurethane, or silicon.

These days, the inert gases argon or krypton, and more rarely xenon, are usually used to fill the air space between the panes, since inert gas improves the insulation of the glass as compared to dehumidified air. It is, however, the <u>coating</u> of the surface of the glass that markedly improves the heat insulation that insulating glass provides.

The effect
of insulating
glass Because the air in the air space of insulating glass is hermetically sealed, differences in pressure between the trapped gas and the atmosphere can cause the panes to bend inward or outward. › Fig. 10

18

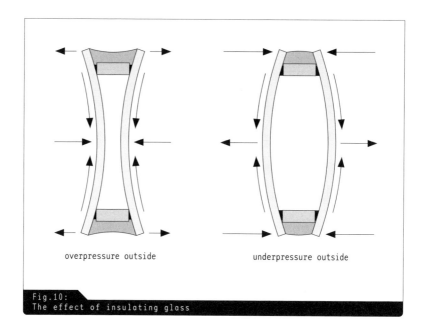

overpressure outside   underpressure outside

Fig.10:
The effect of insulating glass

Consequently, reflections on the pane will be distorted. The differences in pressure result in additional stress on the panes, known as climatic stress. This places strain on the glass and especially the edge seal. In the case of small or very narrow formats in particular, this effect of insulating glass can also cause overstressing and premature failure of the edge seal.

Coating the surface

Coating the surface of the glass can considerably influence the optical and physical properties of the glass, depending on the requirements. In general, metals and metal oxides are used as coating materials. Today, types of glass can be produced that provide insulation or solar control, reflect or do not reflect, provide colors, or repel grime. The thin layers do not affect the structural properties of the glass, but the coatings are often not resistant to environmental influences (corrosion) or mechanical influences (scratching). Thus, many layers, especially those effective as insulation or solar control, can only be applied on the surface of the pane that faces the air space (that is, Surface 2 or Surface 3 in fig. 11). › Fig. 11

The coating is applied either during the manufacture of float glass ("online," as it were) or after manufacture is complete (that is, "offline"). In the online method, liquid metal oxides are applied to the surface of the glass while it is still hot, which binds them to the glass (pyrolysis). The

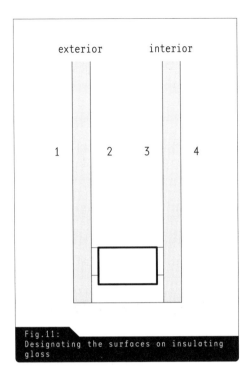

Fig.11:
Designating the surfaces on insulating glass

result is a very resistant layer ("hard coating") that is also suited to the outer surface of the pane (Surface 1 in fig. 11).

Nowadays, most glass for insulation or protection against the sun is produced by the modern <u>cathode ray method</u> (magnetron sputtering), since this method can apply multiple layers that are extreme thin (with thicknesses measured in nanometers). Glass can also be coated using the sol-gel process, in which the glass is dipped multiple times in a chemical solution. After each dipping, the layer absorbed by the surface of the glass is fired.

Designing surfaces

In addition to surface coatings, there are a variety of other treatments for decorating glass surfaces. One popular way of producing custom designs in color is printing on all or part of the surface of the glass. In addition to printing, etching and sandblasting the glass can produce a translucent surface. › Chapter Design glass

SPECIAL-PURPOSE GLASS

THERMAL INSULATING GLASS

The use of insulating glass has become absolutely a matter of course for buildings in cold and moderate climate zones because of energy conservation requirements. In the 1980s glazing was still responsible for high annual heating costs. Today even buildings with generous glazing can have very low or even zero fossil energy usage.

Coefficient
of thermal
conductivity

The unit of measure to indicate the heat loss of building materials, and hence windows and glazing, is the <u>coefficient of thermal conductivity (U-value)</u> in accordance with EN 673. The coefficient of thermal conductivity indicates the flow of warmth passes through 1 m² of a building material with a temperature differential between room and outside air temperature of 1 K (unit = W/m²K). The crucial factors for the insulating properties of a window are, however, the structure of the glass <u>and</u> that of the frame. For that reason, a distinction is made between the U_g-value (g = glazing) of the glazing and the U_w-value (w = window) of the entire window. Because the transfer of heat is generally higher at the edge of the window than in its center, the U_w-value is also higher, and hence poorer, than the U_g-value. U_w is calculated as follows:

$$U_w = \frac{U_g \times A_g + U_f \times A_f + \varphi \times L_g}{A_w} \text{ (W/m}^2\text{K)}.$$

U_w = Coefficient of thermal conductivity of window
U_g = Coefficient of thermal conductivity at center of pane
A_g = Area of glass
U_f = Coefficient of thermal conductivity of window frame
A_f = Area of frame
φ = Linear coefficient of thermal conductivity of edge of glass
L_g = Length of edge of glass
A_w = Area of entire window

The U_g-value of a pane of insulating glass composed of two panes with no coating but air space between them will be approx. 2.8–3.0 W/m²K. If filled with inert gas and coated (generally on Surface 3), by contrast, the U_g-value will be approx. 1.1 W/m²K if filled with argon, or 1.0 W/m²K if filled with krypton. Three-pane insulated glass has a value of about 0.6 W/m²K if filled with argon or 0.5 W/m²K if filled with krypton. › Tab. 3

With insulating glass, one-third of the thermal conductivity results from <u>convection</u> and <u>conduction</u> and as much as two-thirds from <u>radiation</u>. Energy transportation in a gaseous medium is called "convection." Because of the temperature differential between the two panes, the gas

Structure (mm) / Composition	U_g-value (W/m²K)	G-value (%)	Lt-value (%)
Two-pane insulating glass 4/16/4 argon	1.1	63	80
Two-pane insulating glass 4/10/4 krypton	1.0	60	80
Three-pane insulating glass 4/14/4/14/4 argon	0.6	50	71
Three-pane insulating glass 4/12/4/12/4 krypton	0.5	55	72

U_g-value = Coefficient of thermal conductivity of glass

G-value = Solar heat gain coefficient

Lt-value = Light transmittance

The values given here are specific to different manufacturers and hence are not universally valid.

in the air space begins to move and thus transports the warmth from the warm pane to the cold one. Heat conduction is the transportation of energy from a solid body—in this case, the energy flow through the glass—and the edge composite. The thermal radiation of glass panes includes the direct exchange of radiation between the warm glass surface and the cold one. › Fig. 12

Thermal protection coating

The thermal protection coating serves to reduce energy loss from thermal radiation, which is why this layer is also referred to as a <u>Low-E layer</u> (from Low-Emissivity). Silver has become established as the most common coating, as it has not only extremely low emissivity but also high great color neutrality and light transmission. Thermal insulating glass is therefore almost indistinguishable from uncoated insulating glass with the naked eye. › Fig. 13

Condensation

Although insulating glass provides significantly better thermal insulation, <u>condensation</u> can still form on the edge of the surface of the glass on the interior side when external temperatures are low. Over time, the condensation can damage the seal, or the glazing bead in the case of wooden windows. The cause of condensation is the higher thermal conductivity on the edge, since the spacer, which is usually made of metal, is a thermal bridge. Using stainless steel or plastic in place of aluminum for the spacer reduces the <u>linear coefficient of thermal</u>

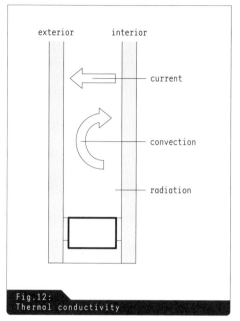

exterior   interior

current

convection

radiation

Fig.12:
Thermal conductivity

Fig.13:
Cigarette lighter test

Solar heat gain
coefficient

conductivity (f) at the edge of the glass and thus reduces condensation and improves the U_w-value of a window by several percent, depending on its dimensions.

One of the essential characteristic values of insulating glass, along with U-value, is <u>solar heat gain coefficient</u> (G-value): G-value (according to EN 410) indicates the total energy admitted of the solar radiation that strikes the glass. The G-value is the sum of the <u>primary transmittance</u> of solar radiation and the fraction of solar radiation absorbed by the glass (<u>secondary transmittance</u>), in the form of thermal radiation and convection. In <u>passive solar buildings</u>, a high G-value is often desirable in order

\\ Tip:
The position of the coating of insulating glass can be determined subsequent to installation by means of the cigarette lighter test. The flame is reflected twice by each pane. The mirror image of the coated surface differs in color from the others (see Fig. 13).

23

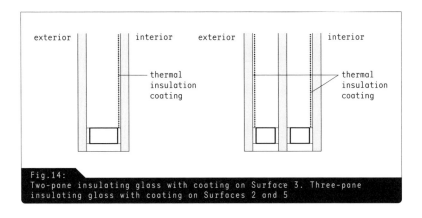

Fig.14:
Two-pane insulating glass with coating on Surface 3. Three-pane insulating glass with coating on Surfaces 2 and 5

to optimize passive solar energy gain. In other types of buildings, such as office buildings with a large percentage of glazing, too much absorption of solar energy poses a risk of overheating the interior. › Chapter Solar control glass

The G-value of thermal insulating glass lies approximately between 0.6 and 0.65. Three-pane insulating glass has a somewhat lower G-value. › Fig. 14

› 🛈

SOLAR CONTROL GLASS

Greenhouse effect

As a transparent building material, glass is permeable to shortwave solar radiation (wavelengths from 300 to 3000 nm) but impermeable to longwave thermal radiation (> 3000 nm). Much of the solar radiation that enters a room is absorbed by the surfaces on which it shines, transformed into heat, and radiated again in the form of longwave thermal radiation. This can no longer be transmitted back outside by the glass, so the room grows continuously warmer. This greenhouse effect means that glazed rooms can overheat even when the outside air temperature is low. › Fig. 15

🛈

\\ Note:
Altering the position of the layer on insulating glass changes the G-value as well. With two-pane insulating glass, the G-value is decreased if the layer is on Surface 2 rather than Surface 3. With three-pane insulating glass, the G-value is higher if Surfaces 3 and 5 are chosen for the layer (rather than 2 and 5). But these measures do not affect U-value.

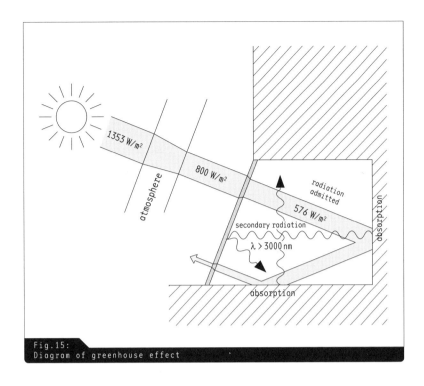

Fig.15:
Diagram of greenhouse effect

Solar control glass prevents much of the radiant energy from entering the room, first, by absorption, and second, by reflection of the radiation that strikes it. Solar control glass was often made of body-tinted glass; it absorbed part of the radiation, which unfortunately included visible light. The earliest types of coated solar control glass had the disadvantage that they reflected much of the visible light.

Selectivity

Modern solar control glass has a <u>selective</u> coating; that is to say, it is transparent to the visible light spectrum but reflects or absorbs long-wave infrared radiation. Today its G-value ranges from about 20 to 50%.

In order to obtain high-quality natural lighting in the interior, it is also important to look for high <u>selectivity</u> (S) when choosing solar control glass. Selectivity is the ratio of <u>light transmission</u> to G-value. For example, if the glazing has a G-value of 40% and allows 76% of visible light through, its selectivity is the quotient of 76:40, or 1.9. The theoretical limit is a value of 2.0.

Color rendering

It is not just the quantity of light that is crucial to the quality of natural light in an interior but also the <u>color rendering. The color rendering index (R_a)</u> should be at least 90%; this is the measure of the rendering of the colors of natural light, measured at the surfaces in the room where

Structure (in mm) / composition	U_g-value (W/m²k)	G-value (%)	LT-value (%)	RA
Single-pane glazing 6 mm				
Clear	5.7	56	45	–
Green	5.7	45	53	–
Two-pane insulating glass Argon Nominal value 68/34	1.1	36	66	–
Two-pane insulating glass Argon Nominal value 40/21	1.1	22	40	88
Two-pane insulating glass 6/16/4 Argon Nominal value blue 50/27	1.1	29	50	95

Tab.4:
Characteristic values of various types of insulating glass

U_g-value = Coefficient of thermal conductivity of glass

G-value = Solar heat gain coefficient

LT-value = Light transmittance

R_a = Color rendering index

The values given here are specific to different manufacturers and hence are not universally valid.

daylight is reflected. The color rendering index (R_a) of glazing can be as high as 99%. > Tab. 4

Diminution factor F_c

In many cases, solar control is also improved by sun shading inside or outside (slats, venetian blinds, awnings, etc.). The solar heat gain

\\Tip:
Solar control glass, including neutral solar control glass, differs according to composition in the degree of reflection and color nuances when viewed from outside (e.g. blue, green, green, or silver). Even when its characteristic values are known, the composition should be sampled prior to installation. This is particularly important when single panes have to be replaced.

Line	Type of shading	F_c
1	No shading	1.0
2	Interior or in air space between panes	
2.1	White or reflective surface with minimal transparency	0.75
2.2	Bright colors or minimal transparency	0.8
2.3	Dark colors or high transparency	0.9
3	Exterior	
3.1	Rotating slats, ventilated behind	0.25
3.2	Venetian blinds and fabrics with minimal transparency, ventilated behind	0.25
3.3	Venetian blinds in general	0.4
3.4	Roller shutters, window shutters	0.3
3.5	Canopies, loggias, free-standing slats	0.5
3.6	Awnings, ventilated above and on the sides	0.4
3.7	Awnings in general	0.5

Tab.5:
Diminution factor F_c

coefficient of the glazing <u>with</u> sun shading is called g_{total}. It is the product of the g-value of the glazing and a diminution factor: › Tab. 5

$$F_c \ (g_{total} = F_c \times g)$$

The G-value of glazing can also be reduced by ceramic printing on (part of) the outer pane of glass. The greater the density or coverage of the printing, the lower the G-value. › Chapter Design glass, Colored glass

SOUNDPROOF GLASS

Architectural projects often have to meet a minimum standard for soundproofing. The degree of soundproofing required depends on the needs of the specific use. A general distinction is made between <u>airborne noise</u> and <u>impact noise</u>. Impact noise is transmitted by walking or pounding directly on parts of the building. Noises transmitted through the air, such as talking or traffic noise, are called <u>airborne noise</u>.

<u>Sound pressure level</u>, measured in decibels (dB), is the unit by which noise is measured. The <u>resultant sound reduction (in dB)</u> of a facade depends essentially on the soundproofing quality of its windows, that is, on the construction of the glass and the frame. Normal insulating glass

already has significantly higher soundproofing than ordinary glass. The following measures can improve the sound reduction index of two-pane insulating glass even more:

– Increasing the quantity of glass and asymmetrical structure (variations in thickness of glass)
– Increasing the air space between panes
– Using laminated safety glass
– Using laminated glass or laminated safety glass (LSG) with special interlayers such as films or cast resin

Soundproofing films meet the same safety requirements (tensile strength and splinter resistance) as traditional PVB films, so that soundproofing glass with cast resin as an interlayer is only rarely used in buildings. Cast resin has only limited tensile strength, and there is a risk that over time it can it can detach and run, becoming visible on the edge of the laminated glass. › Fig. 16

FIRE-RESISTANT GLASS

If a wall is supposed to be flame-retardant or fire-resistant, fire-resistant glass is used in the wall or facade openings. It is important to pay attention to the required fire-resistance rating of the glass according to EN 13501-1. › Tab. 6

The figures indicated in the table show the certified fire-resistance rating of glass. This is the period of time in which glass at least slows the penetration of fumes from fire, indicated in minutes (30 or 90 minutes). E glazing stops only the penetration of fumes, while EI glazing also prevents the penetration of the high thermal radiation from the fire. E glazing can

\\ Note:
The weighted sound reduction index (R_w) is the sound reduction index of a unit for insulating glass that has been measured by an authority recognized in the building code and authenticated with a certificate. The value is calculated in a laboratory and does not take into account the transmittance of sound via adjoining parts of the building. The weighted sound reduction index (R'_w), by contrast, also takes into account the adjoining parts. This value is thus somewhat smaller than the R_w.

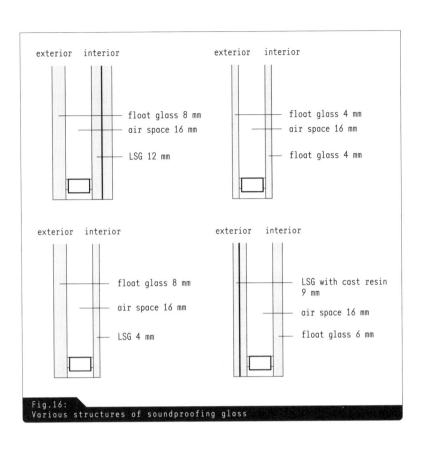

exterior interior

— float glass 8 mm
— air space 16 mm

— LSG 12 mm

exterior interior

— float glass 4 mm
— air space 16 mm

— float glass 4 mm

exterior interior

— float glass 8 mm

— air space 16 mm

— LSG 4 mm

exterior interior

— LSG with cast resin 9 mm

— air space 16 mm

— float glass 6 mm

Fig.16:
Various structures of soundproofing glass

Tab.6:
Classification of fire-resistant glass

Building code designation	Fire-resistance rating according to EN 13501-1
Flame-retardant	EI 30
	E 30
Fire-resistant	EI 90
	E 90

therefore only be used where there is a sufficiently safe distance from people in case of fire—for example, in skylights more than 1.80 m above the floor or in walls that do not adjoin escape routes. Whereas E glazing is monolithic in construction, EI glazing has a multilayer structure composed of normal plate glass and special interlayers that foam up at high temperatures and thus prevent the penetration of fire and heat for the required duration.

SPECIAL TYPES OF SECURITY GLAZING

The spectrum of requirements for glass today also includes protection against vandalism, theft, and violent crime. European standards distinguish between special types of glazing based on the nature and force of the violence against which they provide protection.

Impact-resistant glazing offers protection against stones or smaller projectiles. Such glazing is tested using a falling ball experiment. A steel ball weighing approx. 4 kg is dropped onto the glass three times in a row from a specified height but should not penetrate it.

Burglary-resistant glazing prevents an ax from cutting an opening of 40×40 cm within a specified period. The test is conducted using a long-handled ax attached to a machine.

Bullet-resistant glass, commonly called bulletproof glass, is produced for protection against various firearms, ranging from shotguns to rifles. Such glazing is tested in a laboratory shooting range using common types of firearms.

Blast-resistant glazing protects against attack from outside with explosives. It is tested using an artificially produced pressure wave perpendicular to the glass.

All special security glazing is composed of several layers, ranging from traditional laminated safety glass (LSG) to multilayered structures that consist of glass, tempered glass, films, or even plastic coatings. The focus, however, is always on protecting the people or objects behind the glass. The glass itself is usually damaged when subjected to severe violence and has to be replaced. Security glass can also be fitted with a conductive wire; its current is interrupted when the glass is broken, triggering an alarm. These conductive wires are either thin silver wires inserted into the LSG or conductive enamel printed on one corner of the pane of TSG. Because TSG always breaks into small pieces, the circuit is sure to be broken.

🖇
\\ Note:
To ensure fire safety, all fire-resistant glass must be framed in appropriate constructions in combination with certified materials for connecting and sealing.

INSULATING GLASS WITH INTEGRATED ELEMENTS

One current trend is to integrate functional elements into the air space of insulating glass, for example, slats for shade or metal weave. The advantage of this is that the elements described below are protected from damage by wind and weather and from grime.

Adjustable
systems

Adjustable sunshade slats are integrated venetian blinds made of concave or convex slats with matte, reflective, or perforated surfaces. They can be regulated to provide protection against sun and glare at workplaces with computer monitors.

Adjustable sunshades can also be integrated into the air space. Such blinds are made of textiles or perforated plastic film.

Fixed systems

Fixed sunshade slats are highly reflective, horizontal slats with a special cross section preinstalled in the air space so that most of the direct sunlight is reflected, while diffuse daylight is directed into the room. › Fig. 17

Sunshade grids function like such fixed sunshade slats, except that the slats are arranged vertically and horizontally. Such complex grids, coated with the purest aluminum for reflectivity, were developed especially for use in glass roofs with little slope or for domed roof lights. › Fig. 18

Integrated prism plates or acrylic glass profiles are also used to reflect direct sunlight back out while directing diffuse daylight into the room.

Furthermore, a wide variety of metal weave inserts are available. They not only provide solar control but also emphasize the design. › Fig. 19

Fig.17:
Fixed sunshade slats

Fig.18:
Sunshade grid

Fig.19:
Metal weave insert

Filigree <u>wooden inserts</u> consisting of wood bars of rectangular cross section can be employed in insulating glass instead of metal weave.
› Fig. 20

Finally, mention should be made of other integrated elements that merely scatter light and hence, if thick enough, are also suitable as thermal insulation. <u>Light-scattering capillary plates</u> in insulating glass are made of tiny, UV-stable, transparent polycarbonate tubes that scatter daylight evenly. They are sometimes used for natural lighting in buildings

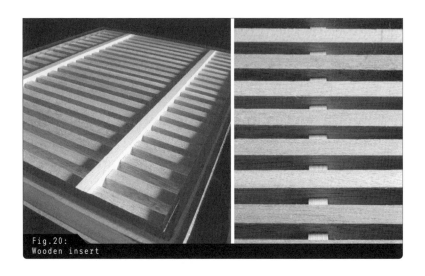
Fig.20:
Wooden insert

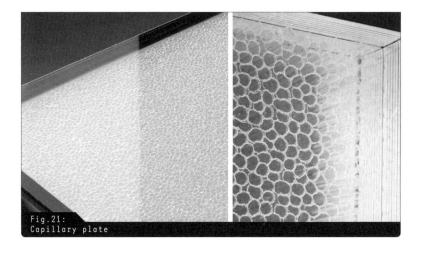
Fig.21:
Capillary plate

where direct lighting is not desirable, for example, in museums, studios, sporting arenas, and so on. › Fig. 21

Transparent thermal insulation

The term <u>transparent thermal insulation</u> is somewhat misleading, since this kind of thermal insulation is usually not transparent at all but merely diffusely translucent. Transparent thermal insulation is often integrated directly in front of a solid exterior wall to provide it with additional winter heating from solar radiation, the energy from which is then transferred to the interior over time. Transparent thermal insulation can

Fig.22:
Photovoltaic element

also be used as infill on the facade in order to profit from additional use of daylight. Materials such as plastic capillary plates, glass tubes with thin walls, or aerogels (foamed granules) are placed between two panes of glass. There should be some means of shading the transparent thermal insulation, however, to avoid overheating the interior on warmer days.

\\ Note:
One disadvantage of integrated elements is that they increase the thermal absorption of the air space between the panes, which can cause premature damage to the elements integrated in the glass. It can be expensive to replace the elements after only a few years. It is also important to ensure that the replacements panes look exactly the same. In integrated venetian blinds, there is also a risk that the double-pane effect (inward curving from climatic stress) on the panes cause the slats to jamb and cease to operate. The bending of the panes can be reduced by using thicker glass.

Fig.23:
Electro-optic functional layer

SPECIAL FUNCTIONAL LAYERS

Its transparency, strength, and resistance to weather make glass an ideal base for many kinds of functional layers.

Photovoltaic

One typical example of special functional layers is <u>photovoltaic elements</u>, which are used in facades or on roofs to transform sunlight into electrical energy. The elements are composed of silicon cells embedded between two panes for protection, or of "thin-film cells," which are produced by coating glass directly. › Fig. 22

Switchable layers

In addition, there are functional layers that, thanks to glass's penetration by light or radiation, can adjust to current lighting or climatic conditions.

<u>Thermotropic functional layers</u> change how much light will penetrate the glazing according to the temperature. They can be set up, for example, so that a pane that seems transparent at room temperature looks white at higher temperatures and hence reflects much of the light diffusely.

<u>Electro-optic functional layers</u> can be switched between diffusely translucent and transparent at the press of a button that applies electricity. › Fig. 23

<u>Electrochromic functional layers</u> are switchable layers that provide continuously adjustable control of the amount of light and energy insulating glasses take in. The pane colors—e.g., turns dark blue—when the electricity is turned on, which reduces the transmission of daylight and solar thermal radiation.

35

Fig.24:
Custom ornamental glass

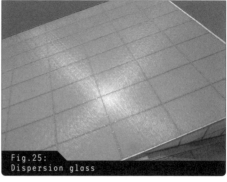

Fig.25:
Dispersion glass

DESIGN GLASS

ORNAMENTAL GLASS

"Ornamental glass" is the term used for cast or rolled glass given a surface structure for functional or design reasons. The variety of possible surfaces ranges from geometric patterns (squares, rectangles, lines, dots) to amorphous patterns and custom ornaments, which can be made to order if quantities are sufficient to justify the effort. › Figs. 24 and 25

Ornamental glass can be slightly or highly diffuse, and it is often used where either diffuse light is desired or clear visibility is undesirable for functional or design reasons. Ornamental glass can be made with either one or both surfaces structured. One special case is glass with a relief surface pattern (e.g. prism glass) that does not scatter daylight diffusely but reflects it or guides it in a particular direction according to the angle of incidence. › Figs. 26 and 27

›

\\Note:
Most types of ornamental glass can be tempered, and many can also be used to make LSG or insulating glass. When it is used for facades, in particular, the manufacturer should be asked to verify this.

Fig.26:
Prism glass

Fig.27:
Using prism glass to direct light

GLASS WITH A FROSTED SURFACE

Frosted glass is a popular design element in architecture, and not without reason. Frosting ensures that the play of light will be interesting, and it heightens the materiality of the glass.

Etching

<u>Etched glass</u> is frosted with hydrofluoric acid. The surface of the glass is damaged only slightly in the process, and hence the strength of the pane is largely preserved. The concentration of acid used today is very low, but this is compensated for by allowing it to work on the surface of the glass for a long time. The duration of application determines the amount of frosting. As the roughness of the surface increases, the transparency of the glass is reduced, since a rough surface will increase the scattering of the light that enters. Stencils can be used to etch individual designs, logos, or patterns. In consultation with the manufacturer, etched glass can be tempered or even bent.

Sandblasting

With <u>sandblasted glass</u>, the surfaced is roughened by sandblasting. Since the surface is damaged by the roughening, the strength of a pane is diminished. Over the course of time, changes in color can result from the roughness of the surface, for example, from grease residue after cleaning. The visual effect is similar to that of etched panes. Images or patterns can also be applied.

Frosting by screen printing is a way to treat the surface without roughening it. A translucent enamel paint is applied and burned in to make it permanent.

COLORED GLASS

Colored glass has recently been enjoying a renaissance in architecture. As early as the Middle Ages, the light in the interiors of Gothic cathedrals was artfully altered by means of tracery windows subdivided into colors. These days there are many kinds of colored glass, with various technical and visual qualities. Depending on the product, the "dyeing process" takes place when the glass is produced or during subsequent processing.

Body-tinted glass

Body-tinted glass is produced by incorporating additives (metal oxides) directly into the glass paste. This method can be used to color float glass, sheet or window glass, and cast glass, as well as glass bricks. The range of colors for float glass is, however, limited to blue, green, bronze, and gray, while the other kinds of glass mentioned have a wider variety of options. Because of the natural iron oxide content in the glass paste, neutral float glass already has a slight green cast—an effect that is more evident when the glass is thick or frosted. White glass is the term for float glass low in iron oxide that has no green cast. Because it is highly transparent, it is also used to produce sun collectors and photovoltaic elements.

Fusing

Fusing is the process of combining glass made from paste of different colors to form a single pane. › Fig. 28 Sheets of glass of various colors and shapes are assembled into a larger sheet and then fused in a kiln at temperatures up to 1500 °C. This technique can be used for sheet glass but not for float glass.

› 🗊

Dichroic glass

Optical effect filters or dichroic filters are thin layers of various metal oxides of different thickness that are applied to glass using the sol-gel method (dipping in a chemical solution). The effect of color results from interference between the individual thin layers and varies according to the angle of incidence of the light. A glass facade of dichroic glass can, for example, reflect sunlight as cobalt blue or gold depending on the angle of incidence. Color effect filters are not very absorbent, that is to say, they will not heat up from solar radiation as much as dyed glass, for example.

› 🗊

Enameled glass

Enameled and screen-printed glass are types of color-coated glass in which a colored enamel layer is burned into the surface of the glass during the production of TSG or LSG (at temperatures over 600 °C). Enameled or

---

🗊

\\ Note:
Body-tinted glass will heat up from solar radiation and thus is often tempered for use in facades. By contrast, plate glass produced by fusing cannot be tempered because its seams are irregular.

🗊

\\ Note:
Dichroic glass is available in sizes up to approx. 1.70 × 3.80 m. Tempering is possible but only within strict limits. The layer is durable and scratch-resistant, but it should not be exposed to weathering.

Fig.28:
Colored glass window of fusing glass

screen-printed glass is thus always tempered; printing without tempering is possible only with organic colors of two components, but it is not scratch-resistant. The best color quality is achieved by using white glass, which is low in iron oxide. It is important to distinguish between the three methods of applying enamel to glass continuously:

_ In the rolling process, the flat pane of glass is passed through a grooved rubber roller that transfers the enamel paint to the surface of the glass.
_ In the casting process, the sheet of glass is passed through a dip coater that covers the surface with paint. This method is outdated and not environmentally friendly, since, unlike the other methods, it is impossible without the use of solvents.

Screen printing   The most uniform application of color is achieved by screen printing. Here the paint is pressed through a fine-mesh screen onto the surface of the glass on the printing table. A wide variety of standard colors is available. These colors include opaque, transparent, and translucent colors as well as custom paints that can be applied either continuously

Fig.29:
Screen-printed glass

Fig.30:
Facade with screen-printed glass

or discontinuously. Using the available decorative patterns and stencils, it is possible to design the glass panes individually. In computer-to-screen (CTS) imaging, the screens are produced from digital designs or photographs. Multicolor printing motifs require a corresponding number of screens and passes. This means, for example, that for a four-color screen print intended to print a photograph on glass, four different screens and passes are required. › Figs. 29 and 30

> 📎

Digital printing

It has recently become possible to print glass with ceramic using digital printing. The advantage is that the data of the image is sent directly to a special printer, and no expensive screens need be produced. Moreover, multiple colors can be applied at the same time. This method is particularly well suited to elaborate custom motifs.

LSG with colored film

LSG with colored interlayers is often used today instead of body-tinted glass made with colored paste. Rather than treating the glass itself, the color is introduced by means of colored films glued between two layers of glass.

A composite of glass, film, and glass behaves like a traditional laminated safety glass, since polyvinyl butyral (PVB) is used as the raw material for the extruded color films. As many as four films can be combined between two sheets of glass. Hence it is possible to generate more than a thousand transparent, translucent, and opaque colors from eleven basic colors. In addition to monochrome and patterned films, there are also films with high-resolution digital printing laminated into LSG. The opacity of the color is, however, lower than that of screen printing on glass. › Fig. 31

> 📎

Holographic films

Holographic optical element (HOE) is a term for laminated glass embedded with films that have holographic grids. HOEs have an effect similar to prisms, in that they break down white light into its spectral colors. The

40

Fig.31:
LSG with patterned film

effect of the color depends on the angle of incidence and the viewing angle. They can produce dynamic color effects, much like the dichroic filters discussed earlier. Holographic optical films can be employed outdoors only if protected within laminated glass. They are used not just for color effects but also to direct daylight and to provide solar control. They are also suited to increasing photovoltaic electricity production by focusing sunlight onto solar cells.

\\ Note:
Enameling reduces the bending strength of TSG by about 40%. Up to four passes in different colors are applied to a surface. Formats up to about 3.00×6.00 m are possible. Custom motifs are more expensive as the custom screens have to be produced. The printed side of the pane is scratch- and weather-resistant, but the color can change over time because of ultraviolet radiation. The printed side of insulating glass is thus usually placed on Surface 2. The color and the amount of printing change in relation to the solar heat gain coefficient of the glazing, which is why screen-printed glass is also used for solar control.

\\ Note:
LSG with color film usually absorbs less warmth than body-tinted glass; nevertheless, with some dark colors it is advisable to temper the individual layers. Protected within the laminate, the colors generally remain stable when exposed to ultraviolet radiation.

CONSTRUCTION AND ASSEMBLY

GENERAL

Because glass is brittle, great care is required, as well as knowledge of materials, when planning and constructing glass structures. Unlike many other <u>tough</u> building materials such as wood or steel, glass can break immediately if it strikes a hard object. For this reason, the bearing capacity of glass components and structures is often carefully tested in a laboratory. This process includes testing their <u>residual bearing capacity</u>—that is, the level of stability and bearing capacity <u>after</u> a break in the glass has occurred. There are many standards, technical guidelines, and regulations on glass and glass constructions. In some countries such as Germany, building <u>nonstandard</u> structures or manufacturing components must be <u>approved on a case-by-case basis</u>.

GLAZING WITH LINEAR SUPPORTS

Glass panes that need to be fastened along a continuous edge are <u>supported linearly</u>. In most cases involving windows, facades, glass roofs, and so on, the glass panes are supported linearly on <u>all sides</u>, or on all edges. They can also be supported on <u>three sides</u>, <u>two sides</u>, or <u>one side</u>.
› Fig. 32 All-glass railings with a lower edge attached to the edge of the roof are one example of a one-sided support system › Chapter Applications, Fall-prevention glazing

Vertical and overhead glazing
A general distinction is made between vertical glazing (tilt angle < 10° from the vertical) and overhead glazing (tilt angle > 10° from the vertical). As a rule, laminated safety glass (LSG) is used for overhead glazing. The PVB film helps prevent shards of glass from falling on people when breakage does occur; LSG made from float glass or HSG also has a much higher residual bearing capacity than monolithic glass. Monolithic glass (such

⓪
\\ Note:
LSG made of TSG may possess high bending strength, but it is not permitted in some countries for overhead areas, because of its poor residual bearing performance. With insulation glass for overhead areas, the bottom glass pane is made of LSG. Wired glass is permitted for overhead areas only where the span of the main load direction is at least 0.7 m.

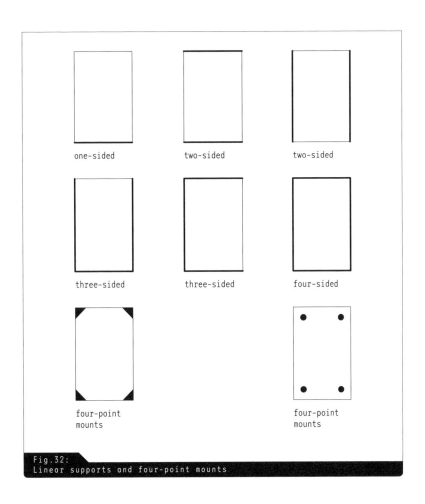

one-sided   two-sided   two-sided

three-sided   three-sided   four-sided

four-point mounts   four-point mounts

Fig.32:
Linear supports and four-point mounts

as float glass, TSG, cast glass) may be used in cases where large pieces of glass falling on public thoroughfares can be otherwise prevented, for example by installing appropriate nets with a mesh width of ≤ 40 mm.

GLASS AND FRAMES

The support needs to have flexible interlayers so as to ensure an even load transfer in the glass panes and to compensate for irregularities. Direct contact with hard materials such as steel or concrete should be avoided at all costs. The glass recess is the specified depth to which the glass extends into the glazing rabbet. The recess is determined by the size of the glass pane, the dimensional tolerance, and the expected deflection of the construction. › Fig. 33

Glazing
rabbet

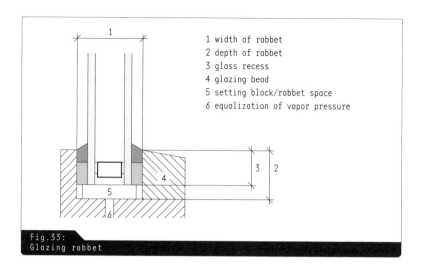

1 width of rabbet
2 depth of rabbet
3 glass recess
4 glazing bead
5 setting block/rabbet space
6 equalization of vapor pressure

Fig.33:
Glazing rabbet

Inserting
setting and
location
blocks

Sealing

Support bolts in the glazing rabbet transfer the vertical load of the glass weight to the sash or frame. In addition, <u>setting blocks</u> in the frame ensure the panes cannot shift sideways. › Fig. 34

The rabbet is now generally constructed without the use of a sealing compound, which guarantees an <u>equalization of vapor pressure</u> (easing of tension) inside it. <u>Caulking</u> is carried out using either a wet sealant applied to a sealing tape (such as silicon, acrylate, polysulfide, or polyurethane), or a dry sealant with a prefabricated gasket profile (such as synthetic rubber). Condensation that collects in the rabbet has to be able to evaporate through small vapor pressure equalization openings. › Fig. 35

It is important to consider the chemical compatibility of the different sealing compounds when planning windows or glass facade structures. There are basically five different classes of sealing compound: butyl, acrylate, polysulfide, polyurethane, and silicon. Sealing compounds vary in their chemical composition, for example in their levels of diluents, solvents, cross-linking agents, and fillers.

›

\\Note:
The wrong sealant compound can cause damage
to the setting and location block material,
edging tape, or sealant material. To assure the
glazing structure's long-term durability, check
the compatibility specifications of the manufacturer's sealant compound.

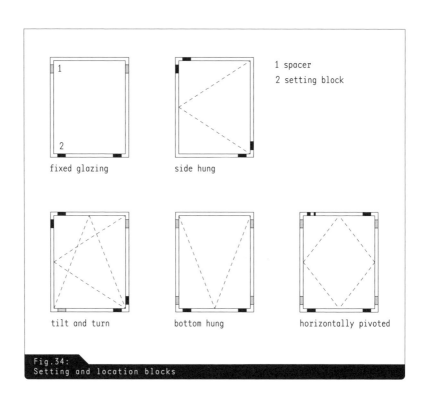

1 spacer
2 setting block

fixed glazing   side hung

tilt and turn   bottom hung   horizontally pivoted

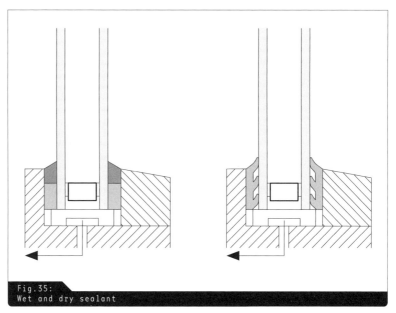

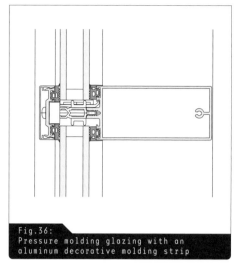

Fig.36:
Pressure molding glazing with an aluminum decorative molding strip

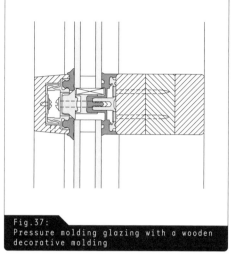

Fig.37:
Pressure molding glazing with a wooden decorative molding

Glazing beads

Glazing with linear supports can be mounted using two essentially different methods. In constructing windows and facade elements, <u>glazing beads</u> are the most common method of fitting glass. The glazing beads are located on the inside of the sash. They are installed either by nails in the support structure (for example with wooden frames) or clamped (in metal or plastic frames). The contact pressure of the glazing beads secures the glass pane mounting and tightens the seal.

Pressure moldings

Pressure moldings are various beads made of aluminum, steel, wood, or plastic that are installed from the outside and press the glass against the substructure. The beads are fixed with screws that allow the contact pressure to be positioned precisely. In most systems the screws are covered by a second molding. The seal is achieved by adding a permanently elastic sealing profile made of silicon or EPDM/APTK. When insulation glass is used in windows it also requires thermal separation between the pressure molding and the support molding, for example by using a plastic insulation molding. As in a window frame rabbet, condensation can also collect in the gap between the glass joints, or rainwater from outside can leak through. For this reason, small holes are required to equalize any vapor pressure. In larger facade constructions, the horizontal and vertical joints are connected to form a <u>communicating drainage system</u>.

The specific material of the pressure molding can be chosen independently of the support profile's material, yet the advantages and disadvantages of each material should be weighed in relation to one other. Aluminum is more resistant to corrosion than steel, for example, and the

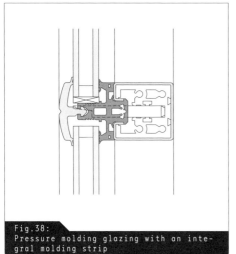

Fig.38:
Pressure molding glazing with an inte-
gral molding strip

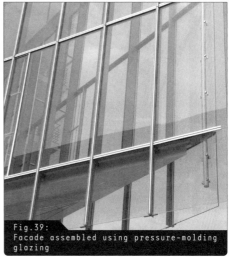

Fig.39:
Facade assembled using pressure-molding
glazing

extrusion press production method makes it easier to manufacture. It should nonetheless be combined with an aluminum covering to protect it from erosion.

One particular form of pressure molding is called <u>integral molding</u>. This is a permanently elastic, synthetic molding that combines the functions of a pressure molding and a sealing profile. › Figs. 36–39

GLAZING WITH POINT MOUNTING SUPPORTS

One benefit of this type of assembly is its ability to deliver very delicate and transparent glass surfaces. With point mounts, the glass pane is not supported along the entire side but only at specific points. Rectangular or square glass panes are attached on at least all four corners; larger formats are additionally anchored to a substructure by point mounts. The local tension in the glass can be very great; tempered glass (TSG or HSG) is therefore generally recommended and sometimes even required. There are two different types of point mount fasteners: <u>clamp mounts</u>, which do not penetrate the glass, and fasteners that require a borehole in the glass.

Clamp mounts

<u>Clamp mounts</u> secure the pane by clamping the glass corners and/or edges. They are made of aluminum or stainless steel and are available in a range of square to round shapes. › Figs. 40–44

During the planning and constructing phase, it is important to note that any direct contact between metal and glass should be avoided by using elastic intermediary layers. Strain due to canting or too much contact pressure from the fixtures can cause the glass to break and should be

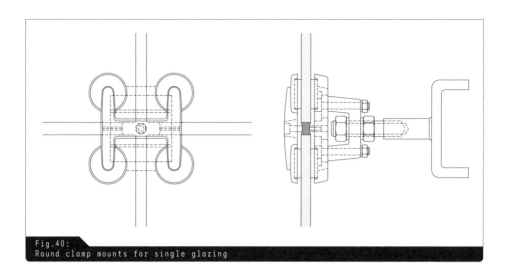

Fig.40:
Round clamp mounts for single glazing

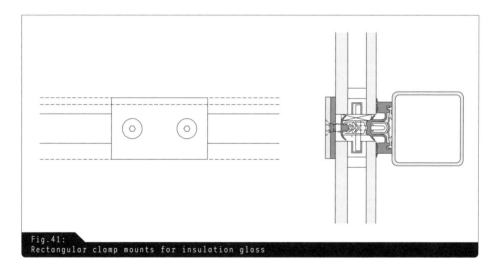

Fig.41:
Rectangular clamp mounts for insulation glass

avoided at all costs. Clamp mounts are also often custom made for building projects. According to the construction of the clamp mount, glass panels can either be flush-mounted or scaled. The clamped area covering the glass should be no smaller than 1000 mm^2 (with at least a 25 mm glazing rabbet recess) and is determined by the amount of glass tension expected. Since this method does not call for boreholes to be made in the glass, the clamp mounts are bolted together in the joints between the glass panes.

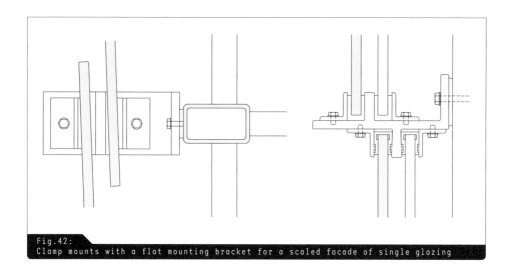

Fig.42:
Clamp mounts with a flat mounting bracket for a scaled facade of single glazing

Fig.43:
Facade with clamp mounts

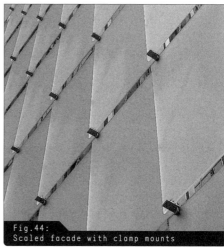

Fig.44:
Scaled facade with clamp mounts

Point mount glazing clamps can also be combined with a linear support. In this method the glass pane rests on a continuous supporting molding and is pressed by a clamp plate against the molding at particular intervals.

Point mounts in the borehole

<u>Point mounts in the borehole</u> secure the glass pane from within the glass surface. The boreholes required for this glazing system make it more labor-intensive than the clamp mount method. Point mounts are available

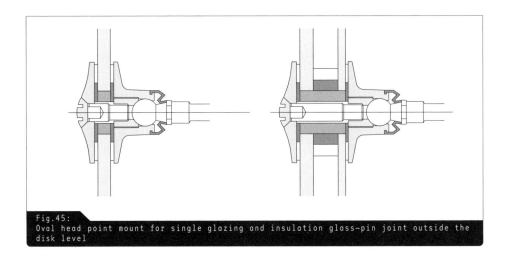

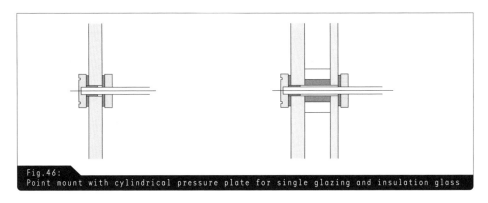

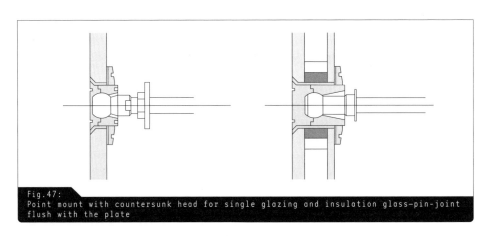

Fig.48:
Facade with point mounts

in various forms: flush point mounts (flat head) and point mounts with attached pressure disks (clamp plates), for example, in lenticular (oval head)
or cylindrical shapes. > Figs. 45–48

This system requires a precise static and structural plan, since the
area of glass near the face of the hole is already damaged, and therefore
weakened by drilling, and since this area also has to withstand the great-
est tension under strain. The minimum spacing between boreholes or between boreholes and the exposed edge of the glass should not be less than
80 mm. For insulation glass, an additional edge seal is required around the
drill hole to ensure the area between the glass panes remains watertight.
Point mounts inside boreholes are elaborate and time-consuming to develop; it is common to use patented and approved production models for
glass facades and roofs.

One special form of point mounting is the <u>undercut anchor</u>. This fas-
tens the glass on one side only, and does not need to be bolted from the
other side. The glass is fixed to the support by clamping a ductile cylinder
in a conical borehole in the glass. > Fig. 49

Undercut
anchors

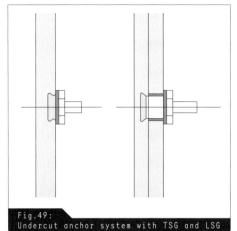

Fig.49:
Undercut anchor system with TSG and LSG

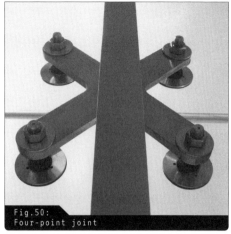

Fig.50:
Four-point joint

Point mounts with an integrated spherical joint are often used for glass facade structures, which helps avoid greater stress on the points caused by a bowing of the glass pane. Point mounts are fixed by stud bolts onto a substructure. Substructures and stud bolts should allow for subsequent settling of the glass panes and compensate for dimensional tolerance. A flush, steel profile with a slotted hole, for example, or a special four-point joint of stainless steel is appropriate for this system. › Fig. 50

GLASS JOINTS AND GLASS CORNERS

Glass joints

If no cover molding is available, the glass edge of a point mount glazing is exposed. In a single glazing system with limited weather protection, such as a multistory parking garage or warehouse, the glass joints can remain open. Such facades are more cost-effective to build and also guarantee good ventilation. Yet it is necessary to seal the joints of insulation glass facades. The joints also have to be elastic, since glass expands from warming (dilatation) and facades can bow in the wind.

Sealing moldings

There are two basic different types of sealing profiles. The first involves pressing a sealing profile of EPDM/APTK or silicon into the joints. The second involves applying a spray sealant to the sealing profile, which seals the joints from the outside. › Figs. 51 and 52 In insulating or laminated glass, the rabbet should remain open to allow vapor pressure equalization and drainage, and thus guarantee the long-term durability of the edges of the glass. This method ensures that water from leakage or condensation does not remain too long in one place and can be quickly transferred outside via the drainage system. The exposed edge seal of the insulation glass must be UV resistant. A UV-resistant edge seal can be made by using

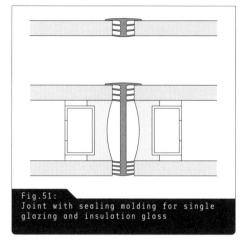

Fig.51:
Joint with sealing molding for single
glazing and insulation glass

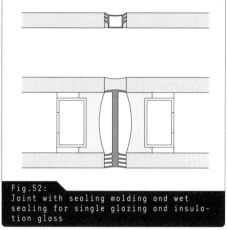

Fig.52:
Joint with sealing molding and wet
sealing for single glazing and insulation glass

silicon (rather than polysulfide or polystyrene) in second-phase sealing, or by means an enamel strip, usually black, pressed into the inner side of the outer glass pane (Surface 2) and covering the edge seal.

Glass corners   The principle for glass corners is similar to that for glass joints. Vapor pressure equalization and the chemical compatibility of the sealant must be checked and guaranteed. The insulation qualities of glass corners are less favorable than the glazing itself, and condensation build-up should therefore be expected. There are diverse possible ways of constructing a glass corner with frameless glazing using insulation glass. The following solutions are the most common:

_ Opaque corners: the corner is filled with an insulation molding
  › Fig. 53
_ Stepped insulating glass with outer edges mitered › Fig. 54
_ Stepped insulating glass, slotted together › Fig. 55

The forms for implementing stepped insulation, especially with a mitered edge, are more complicated and call for precise assembly and joints. The advantage, however, is that the view of the continuous glass surface is not interrupted by another material even in the corners.

STRUCTURAL SEALANT GLAZING (SSG)

Structural sealant glazing constructions are systems where the glass pane is attached by adhesive. This special form of linear support is not automatically approved; therefore the chosen system requires individual authorization under building law. Gluing the glass panes onto a metal frame

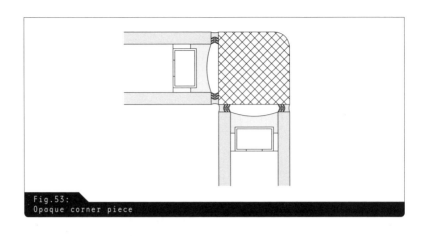

Fig.53:
Opaque corner piece

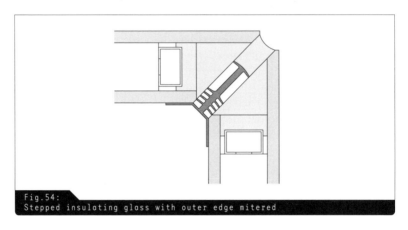

Fig.54:
Stepped insulating glass with outer edge mitered

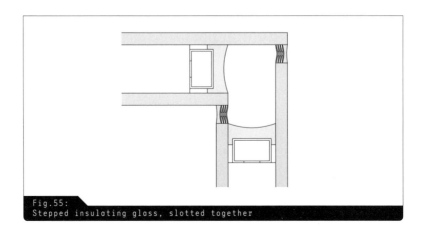

Fig.55:
Stepped insulating glass, slotted together

(adapter frame), which is also fixed to a support profile, provides a flush, frameless facade surface.

Bonding is resistant to wind load; the weight of the glass is supported by the "classic" setting and location blocks system. All-around bonding cannot be carried out at the building site. It requires a licensed factory with a precise climate- and temperature-controlled environment that is also free of dust and debris. In most cases, bonding is done in the glass factory directly after the glass is produced. The glass panes must be absolutely clean, dry, and free of grease.

In some countries such as Germany, glazing more than 8 m high requires an additional wind suction safeguard made of metal. It protects against falling glass if the bond fails. Great demands are made on the bond; it must withstand diverse loads, such as change in temperature, humidity, UV light, and possible corrosion due to microorganisms. The additional suction safeguard is required because it is very difficult to ascertain the long-term bearing capacity of the bond construction method. The suction safeguard can be mounted as an all-around frame, or point mounted. There are different systems for SSG facades for applying the bond, suction safeguards, joint sealant, and insulation glass, which is either step-mounted (stepped insulation glazing) or has a bluntly cut edge. > Figs. 56–58

The bond is compatible with silicon and polyurethane, among others. As is the case with point mounted glazing, SSG glazing also needs to be UV protected on the exposed edge bond. Bond constructions are increasingly being used for SSG glazing as well as all-glass structures. They also have the capacity to assume important structural functions. > Chapter Applications

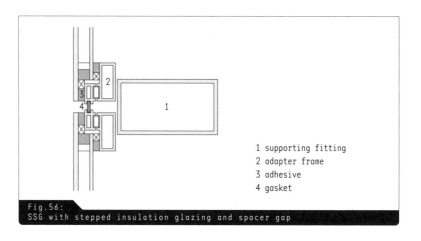

1 supporting fitting
2 adapter frame
3 adhesive
4 gasket

Fig.56:
SSG with stepped insulation glazing and spacer gap

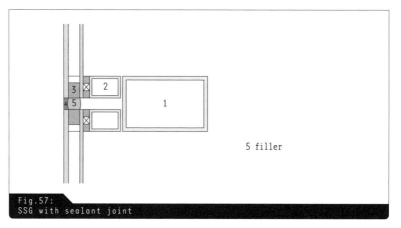

5 filler

Fig.57:
SSG with sealant joint

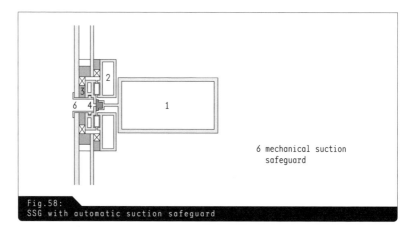

6 mechanical suction
  safeguard

Fig.58:
SSG with automatic suction safeguard

APPLICATIONS

VERTICAL GLAZING

Whereas only certain types of glass are permitted for overhead glazing, › Chapter Construction and assembly theoretically any kind of glass can be used for vertical glazing. In practice, however, there are limitations based on the place it is installed, its use, and its construction.

Types of glass, risk of breakage

Toughened safety glass (TSG) or laminated safety glass (LSG) is often used in place of float glass to minimize the risk of accident. It is necessary to use safety glass, for example, in circulation areas in schools and kindergartens unless other measures, such as handrails or balustrades, have been taken to prevent people from colliding with the glass. Sometimes TSG is also used as an outer glazing for insulating glass to reduce the risk of glass breakage: this is particularly true of facades located above public circulation areas, or when the glass cannot be framed on all sides. For simple glazing that does not have linear mounts on all sides, the use of HSG, TSG, LSG, or if necessary wired glass, is recommended instead of float glass. In many countries this is even required. When glass is installed at a height above 4 m, toughened glass that has been heat soak tested is used instead of ordinary TSG to avoid spontaneous breakage from inclusions of nickel sulfide. › Chapter Glass as a building material

Point-supported glazing usually requires the use of tempered glass. When glass is installed at a height above 4 m, it is common to use laminated safety glass composed of two-pane TSG or two-pane HSG to prevent individual pieces from falling when the glass is damaged.

Load bearing, size of elements

Apart from design and functional criteria, the sizes of element are depend on the loads, the type of mounting, and the type of glass used. When calculating vertical glass elements, in addition to the weight of the elements themselves, wind load (wind suction and wind pressure), climate (for insulating glass › Chapter Glass as a building material), and especially traffic load (e.g. horizontal impact stresses in the case of store

---

\\Tip:
Glass with highly absorbent (solar control) coatings or body-tinted glass will be warmed by the sun more than neutral, colorless glass and should therefore be tempered. That applies above all to panes of glass that absorb more than 50% of incoming thermal radiation.

Fig.59:
Installing a large pane of insulating glass at a construction site

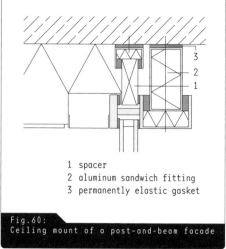

1 spacer
2 aluminum sandwich fitting
3 permanently elastic gasket

Fig.60:
Ceiling mount of a post-and-beam facade

windows) must be taken into account. Theoretically, using linear mounting on all sides, single-pane glazing and even insulating glazing as large as 3.21 × 6.00 m (ribbon size) could be installed. For linear mounting on fewer than four sides or for point mounting, the largest possible formats are considerably smaller than that, since they have to absorb greater bending and higher tension in the glass. The weight of the glass limits size even further: a pane of insulating glass von 3 × 6 m in size can easily weigh as much as 2 t. The installation of large and heavy plates of glass is complicated and requires heavy-duty <u>vacuum lifters</u> to hoist the glass. › Fig. 59

Facade types

In essence, two types of glass facades are distinguished: post-and-beam facades and modular facades.

The term post-and-beam refers to the bearing structure of the facade, which consists of vertical elements (posts) and horizontal ones (beams). The individual posts and beams are assembled on site by welding or screwing them together. Then the glass is fastened to this substructure from outside. The post-and-beam facade makes it possible to build large spans but has the disadvantage that the onsite assembly is more complicated and takes more time than modular facades require.

Modular facades consist of elements prefabricated in the factory into which all the structural elements, such as frame, glazing, and casements, are already integrated. › Chapter Applications, Openings The dimensions of the prefabricated elements have to be suitable for transportation, which limits the size of the elements available.

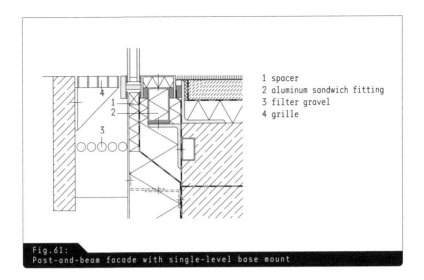

1 spacer
2 aluminum sandwich fitting
3 filter gravel
4 grille

Fig.61:
Post-and-beam facade with single-level base mount

Mounting
details

The mounts of a glass for attaching a glass facade to adjoining build-ing parts, such as the roof or floor structure, have to be constructed in a way that they do not cause additional load on the glass panes in the glaz-ing unit.

Roof mount,
ceiling mount

For that reason, the facade in the glazing unit is attached to the ceil-ing using a plastic <u>spacer</u> or an <u>aluminum sandwich fitting</u>. Traffic load or movements of the roof caused by settling are stabilized by such <u>flexible</u> mounts. The seal and the thermal separation of the facade are preserved.
> Fig. 60

Base mount

A spacer is also used for the <u>base mount</u> of a post-and-beam facade; it is attached together with waterproofing to the lower beam of the facade and fastened behind the pressure molding. It is important that the point where the seal and facade are attached be at least 15 cm above the layer that conducts the water. With a single-level mount on the exterior, a gutter is vital to ensure drainage. > Fig. 61

OPENINGS

<u>Openings</u> in a building's shell have essential functions to fulfill. Moreover, their design is especially important for the overall look. In the case of glass facades, openings are also important because they help reg-ulate the climate in the building. They permit natural ventilation of the interior and thus help keep solar radiation from continually warming of the air. In addition to classic casement windows, additional opening ele-ments are employed in glass facades and glass roofs to ensure continuous

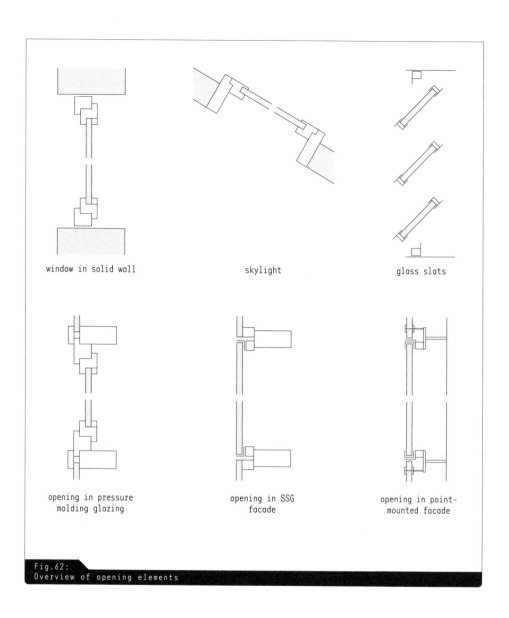

window in solid wall	skylight	glass slats
opening in pressure molding glazing	opening in SSG facade	opening in point-mounted facade

Fig.62:
Overview of opening elements

ventilation; they can be automatically controlled according to room temperature. Various types of openings in glass facades are listed and described below. › Fig. 62

The window element in a wall is the simplest and the original form of glass facade. It can be composed of a single field or be divided into several, which can in turn have either fixed glazing or panes that open (sashes).

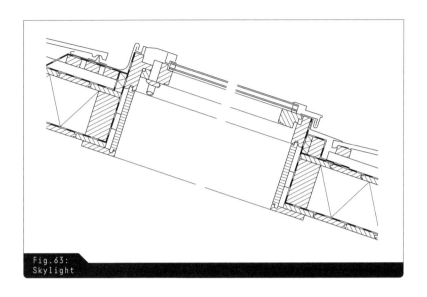

Fig.63:
Skylight

The <u>skylight</u> provides light and ventilation for rooms under ceilings. The glass has to meet the requirements for overhead glazing. The skylight should always be installed at an angle to ensure unrestricted water drainage. › Fig. 63

<u>Glass slats</u> or slat windows make it possible to set precisely the required <u>ventilation cross section</u> and hence regulate the ventilation of the room. Slats are available in various types, with and without frames, for single-pane and insulating glass. › Figs. 64 and 65

The openings discussed above can also be integrated into pressure molding glazing. The glass of the window frame of the opening element is replaced by a supporting frame and pressure molding, which are then clearly visible from the outside.

\\Tip:
More on the theme openings may be found in Roland Krippner and Florian Musso, *Basics Facade Apertures*. Basel: Birkhäuser Verlag, 2008.

\\Tip:
Slats of single-pane glass are used for adjustable, exterior sunshades. The surface of the glass is printed or coated for that purpose. With the addition of integrated solar cells, electricity can be produced to operate the glass slats.

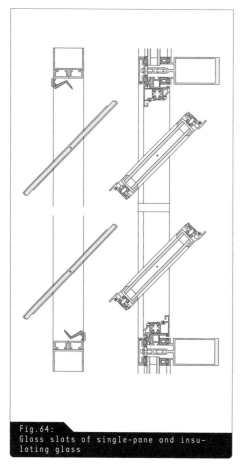

Fig.64:
Glass slots of single-pane and insulating glass

Fig.65:
Window with glass slots

For openings in SSG facades, <u>top-hung sashes</u> that open outward are used. This solution provides for openings with frameless views outward, which are very attractive in SSG facades. › Fig. 66

The integration of opening elements in point-mounted glazing is a special challenge, since the filigree appearance of the facade should not be disturbed in the area of the windows either. For facades with single-pane glazing, for example, top-hung sashes or slats of point-mounted glass can be employed.

Facades of insulating glass require considerably more effort. Because of the lack of frame, the possibilities for attaching seals and fittings that will provide sufficient thermal insulation are very limited. It is possible, for example, to install top-hung sashes as on SSG facades.

Fig.66:
Openings in SSG facade

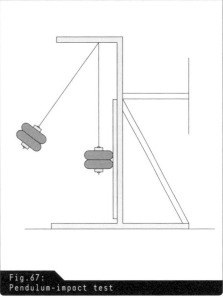

Fig.67:
Pendulum-impact test

FALL-PREVENTION GLAZING

Glass structures used in place of a banister or balustrade required under the building code to prevent people from falling are called fall-prevention glazing. The spectrum of applications ranges from balustrade infill of glass by way of all-glass balustrades to glazing the full height of the room with linear or point mounts. In many countries, the security of fall-prevention glazing has to be demonstrated by a dynamic stress test such as the <u>pendulum-impact test</u>. › Fig. 67

Because such testing is quite complicated, the structure should be planned so that experience from tried-and-tested constructions is applied and further stress testing can be avoided. Glazing that prevents falls can be divided into three categories:

Fixed
full-height
glazing

The first is fixed full-height glazing—that is, glazing without opening sashes, handrails, or protruding rails to support horizontal loads. Linear mounts on all sides are the most effective solution from a structural perspective. If this is not possible, the free edges of the glazing have to be protected from impact in other ways, such as adjoining panes of glass or neighboring architectural elements such as walls or ceilings. Panes of glass mounted on two sides will bend considerably more in case of impact because two edges are free. Care should therefore be taken to inset the glass sufficiently, so that the pane cannot slide out of the holder. In the

Fig.68:
All-glass balustrade

Fig.69:
Banister with point-supported glass infill

› 🔒 ✎

Fixed, bearing
balustrade

case of point mounting, the clamp plates must have a diameter of at least 50 mm.

The second category includes bearing glass balustrades that have linear mounts on their bottom edge with a clamp construction. The upper edge should be protected against impact, for example, with a fitting applied with adhesive or a continuous mounted handrail. The latter should be of appropriate size to ensure that if one pane fails the horizontal load will be transferred to the next pane. The appropriate type of glass for this category is LSG made of HSG or TSG. › Fig. 68

Balustrade
infill

The third and last category is balustrade glass in facades and glass banisters in which glass is used as infill. The horizontal loads are supported by a bearing handrail or a crossbar (facade). The glazing has either point mounts or linear mounts on at least two opposite sides. The panes

› 🔒

should be either LSG or TSG. › Fig. 69

🔒

\\ Note:
In most cases, fall-prevention glazing calls for the use of laminated safety glass, and in the case of point mounting, LSG made from HSG or TSG. If the pane is broken, the laminate of glass and highly tear-resistant film still offers sufficient protection for the person colliding with it.

✎

\\ Tip:
One special case is fixed full-height glazing with a bearing rail whose height is specified in the building code, for example, a round stainless steel fitting on the inside, which will largely absorb any stress from impact. Here, the thickness of the glass can be reduced without altering its outward appearance.

OVERHEAD GLAZING

Overhead glazing, like vertical glazing, can have either linear or point mounts.

Bearing loads, dimensions

Structural loads on overhead glazing is higher than on vertical glazing, since the pane's own weight runs perpendicular to its plane, and because wind, climate, and snow loads have to be taken into account as well. Because of these increased stresses, the format of the elements cannot be as large in overhead areas as on facades. For larger glass roofs, additional loads for people and material have to be assumed as well, since it has to be possible to walk on the glazing for maintenance and cleaning. › Chapter Applications, Glazing for restricted and unrestricted foot traffic

In addition, a glass roof should be resistant to impact, which can result from hailstones or falling branches, for example. Tempered glass should therefore be used as the upper layer on a glass roof. For point-mounted overhead glazing, the required thickness depends not only on loads but also on residual bearing capacity. The same is true of the diameter of the clamp mounts. › Tab. 7

Tab. 7:
Point-mounted overhead glazing with certified residual bearing capacity with rectangular grid of supports

Diameter of clamp mounts (mm)	Minimal thickness of glass (mm) LSG made of HSG	Spacing of supports (cm) in direction 1	Spacing of supports (cm) in direction 2
70	2 × 6	90	75
60	2 × 8	95	75
70	2 × 8	110	75
60	2 × 10	100	90
70	2 × 10	140	100

\\ Note:
In the case of glass enclosures of elevator shafts or escalators, additional measures are usually necessary to ensure the safe operation of the conveyor system. For example, the glazing should be installed in such a way that it is not possible to reach over or between the plates of glass (in the case of frameless glazing).

\\ Note:
For point-mounted overhead glazing, the minimum requirement is LSG consisting of 2×6 mm thick HSG and PVB film at least 1.52 mm thick. The diameter of the clamp plates should be at least 60 mm. The free edge of the glass—that is, the distance between the edge of the glass and the point mount—has to be at least 80 mm and may be at most 300 mm.

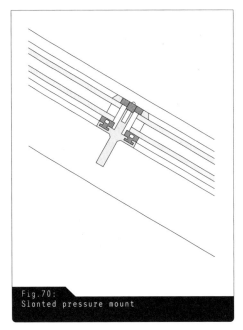

Fig.70:
Slanted pressure mount

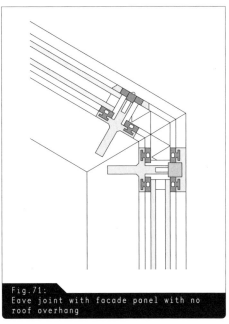

Fig.71:
Eave joint with facade panel with no
roof overhang

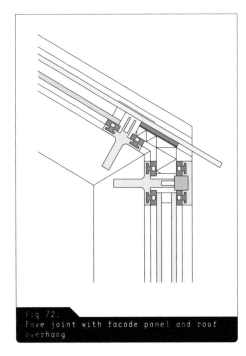

Fig.72:
Eave joint with facade panel and roof
overhang

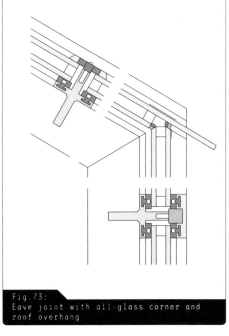

Fig.73:
Eave joint with all-glass corner and
roof overhang

The glass surface should always have sufficient slope leading to the level where water is directed, that is, to a drainage gutter or an adjoining flat roof. Pressure moldings (pressure molding glazing) should installed at an angle so the water can run off. › Fig. 70

The eave joint with attachment to a vertical glazing can be constructed with or without an overhang. If there is no overhang, the rainwater runs directly down the facade, dirtying it. Larger glass roofs should therefore be drained via gutters. › Figs. 71–73

GLAZING FOR RESTRICTED AND UNRESTRICTED FOOT TRAFFIC

Overhead glazing that has to be stepped on for maintenance and cleaning is referred to as <u>step-on glazing</u>. It should be noted that, despite the name, only a limited number of maintenance people can step on the glass at the same time. In addition to the structural strength of the glass, it is necessary to plan measures to avoid slipping. If the slope of the roof is greater than 20°, safety hooks should be installed. The glazing itself should be LSG with certified impact resistance and residual bearing capacity. With insulating glass, the upper pane can be TSG rather than LSG.

<u>Glazing for unrestricted foot traffic</u> can, unlike glazing for restricted foot traffic, also be accessed by the public, and hence it is subject to considerably higher traffic load. Usually a maximum of 5.0 KN/m^2 is assumed. Walk-on glazing typically employs LSG approx. 30 mm thick or more. The glazing is often composed of three individual panes, with the upper pane of TSG or HSG to provide an impact-resistant surface and to protect the two lower panes from damage. The bearing function is fulfilled by the two lower panes, which is why the glazing will remain strong enough for standing on even if the covering pane is damaged. › Fig. 74

The surface should be made skid-proof, either by means of special ceramic screen printing that offers a rough surface on all or part of the glass. A rough, skid-proof surface can also be produced by etching. Glazing that will be walked on usually has linear mounts on two or four sides. In the former case, it must also be bolted to the supporting structure. With an insert of at least 30 mm, panes of glass rest on pressure-resistant elastomer supports. Glass-to-glass or glass-to-metal contact on the sides is prevented by inserting spacers. Glazing suitable for foot traffic is used, for example, for interior stairs of floor structures. Construction solutions for insulated glass suitable for foot traffic are complicated, since high traffic loads cannot be shifted to the edge assembly, as it can with glass suitable for light traffic, since the edge assembly would be damaged by the constant strain. Glass suitable for light traffic, which is used for example to illuminate exhibition areas in museums, is therefore often

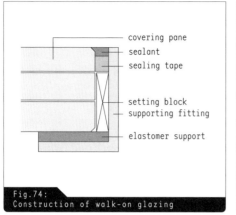

covering pane
sealant
sealing tape

setting block
supporting fitting

elastomer support

Fig.74:
Construction of walk-on glazing

Fig.75:
Glazing for unrestricted foot traffic

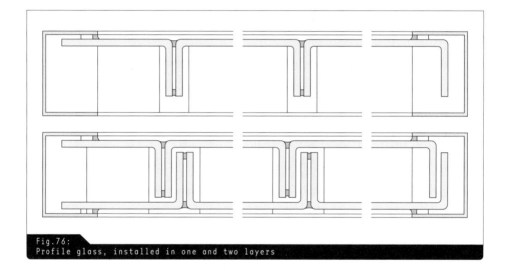

Fig.76:
Profile glass, installed in one and two layers

constructed as a two-layer roof. The insulating glass required for thermal separation is thus on the second layer beneath the glass suitable for light traffic. > Fig. 75

PROFILE GLASS

The advantage of profile glass is that there is no need for a substructure on the facade to bear the load. Rigid glass profiles make it possible to install glass across large surfaces without using muntins. Profile glass

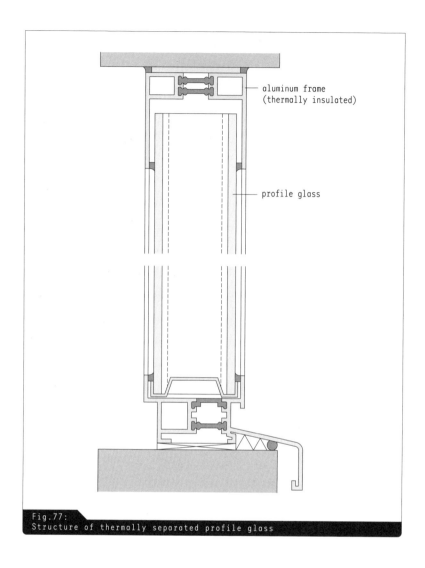

aluminum frame
(thermally insulated)

profile glass

Fig.77:
Structure of thermally separated profile glass

can be installed vertically or horizontally. For purposes of attachment and load transfer, the profiles are inserted into the narrow sides of an approx. 50 mm deep aluminum frame. They can be installed in one or two layers.
> Fig. 76

Thermal separation

A thermally separated glass facade is only possible with two-pane glass. The glass profiles are then installed facing one another. Then setting blocks and sealant are applied to the joints. With a two-layer facade, it also makes sense to have a thermally separated frame. > Fig. 77

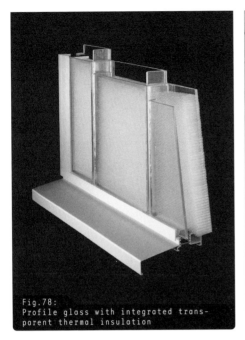

Fig.78:
Profile glass with integrated transparent thermal insulation

Fig.79:
Example of facade with profile glass

Because the space between the glass profiles cannot be dehumidified as it can with insulating glass, an opening to the outside has to be planned to avoid condensation by permitting the damp air to escape. Profile glass can be tempered, which improves its structural characteristics and safety. Tempered profile glass can be as long as approx. 7 m. In addition, wire can be rolled in when the glass is manufactured to provide protection against splintering. Such profiles cannot, however, be tempered.

Surface design, coating

Various kinds of surface designs can be manufactured on profile glass, from smooth to patterned. As a result of the manufacturing process, however, the surface of smooth profile glass is not as even as that of float glass, which clearly detracts from the quality of its transparency. › Fig. 80 Profile glass is now available in coated versions as well, for example, with coatings for thermal insulation or solar control. On a two-layer glazing with profile glass, the coating for thermal insulation is placed on the inner layer, while the coating for solar control is on the outer layer. It is also possible to integrate transparent thermal insulation into profile glass. › Figs. 78 and 79

This is done by placing a capillary insert in the air space between the panes to scatter natural light. This effect is used above all for buildings that will benefit from even, glarefree distribution of light, such as sports arenas, workshops, museums, and studios.

Fig.80:
Transparent profile glass

Fig.81:
Glass supporting structure with
linearly mounted glass facade

Fig.82:
Glass supporting structure with point-
mounted glass facade

Fig.83:
Supporting grid of glass

GLASS SUPPORTING STRUCTURES

The dematerialized structures of our age reflect the technical advances of recent decades concerning glass as a building material. Glass in
buildings is no longer limited to serving as a shell but has begun to take
over supporting functions. Glazing for unrestricted foot traffic has already
been introduced, but its substructure is not usually made of glass. Since
the 1990s, however, glass buildings have been building employing glass as
the primary building material for the supporting structure. That means
that the supports or posts of a glass facade, which provide reinforcement
and absorb wind loads, are also made of glass.

Beams of flat
glass

Rather than steel or wooden profiles, slender blades, for example,
of laminated safety glass form the supporting structure. As with facades,
the supporting members of a roof can also be made of glass. This ensures
maximum transparence and lighting of a covered courtyard or interior.

> Figs. 81–83

Fig.84:
Glass footbridge connecting two buildings

Fig.85:
Detail of the footbridge

Increasingly innovative constructions are constantly expanding the number of all-glass buildings. For example, there are glass connecting bridges, all-glass stairways, experimental supports of glass tubes, and arch and shell supporting systems. > Figs. 84–87

Bearing glass tubes

Tubes of borosilicate glass have a cross section with good structural properties and are particularly well suited to absorbing high compressive forces. They can replace supports of concrete, steel, or wood in buildings. Particular attention must be paid to the steel parts on the ends of the tubes, which have to distribute the forces evenly over the cross section of the tube. The load is transferred to adjoining parts of the building by means of a ball joint, which prevents the shear forces and bending moments from being transferred to the cross section of the glass.

Shell and arch supporting structures

Especially for supporting structures that are primarily subject to compressive forces and not bending moments, such as supporting structures in the form of arches, domes, or shells, glass, with a compressive strength much higher than its tensile strength, can demonstrate its capabilities.

Calculating glass supporting structures

The prerequisites for the development described were, first, new possibilities of processing sheet glass into TSG, HSG, or multilayer LSG, which considerably improved the bearing and residual bearing capacity of such

Fig.86:
Glued glass stair construction

Fig.87:
Detail of glued stair construction

constructions. Second, this progress in the most recent methods was due to the predetermination of the bearing behavior of glass through experiment and calculation. In contrast to ductile materials like steel, which can reduce high tensions by distorting plastically, points of high tension will cause glass to break spontaneously. The load limit of a specific pane of glass is difficult to determine, because it depends on how much it has already been damaged (scratches, small breaks on the edges). The tensions permitted are therefore often much lower than the actual load limit of the pane. This ensures sufficient protection against spontaneous breakage, but it also means that all-glass constructions cannot be quite as delicate as would theoretically be possible.

Connectors

The particular difficulty of all-glass constructions is usually not redirecting forces in the sheet of glass itself but rather transferring them from one component to the next. In the region of such transfer points, the joint is either made by means of classical mechanical connectors (point or clamp mounts) or through adhesive connections. Adhesive connections have the advantage that they permit a uniform (and hence suited to the material) distribution of load to the glass. The transfer of load to the adhesive surfaces can, however, be diminished by outside influences such as dampness, temperature, or aging. In practice, therefore, silicon adhesives are usually employed, although research is currently being conducted on other suitable adhesives with greater strength, such as hot melt adhesive foils.

Glass beams are made of laminated glass, usually composed of three or more panes of TSG or HSG. The outer panes provide protection, while the inner ones provide the actual support. At present, there are no universal regulations for such constructions, so that the building codes differ greatly from country to country.

The technological limits of all-glass structures are determined not only by the strength of the materials but also by the possibilities for manufacturing them. Most processing plants can produce laminated safety glass up to 7 m long, and as thick as 80 mm. Greater lengths require an autoclave capable of handling special sizes, something few companies have.

IN CONCLUSION

The visions of Bruno Taut (Haus des Himmels [House of the Sky], 1920) or Ludwig Mies van der Rohe (glass high-rise project, Berlin 1921) testify to the fascination that glass has for architects. Nearly ninety years later, the building material of modernism has not ceased to be a modern building material.

Because of climate change, the ecological responsibility of architects is greater than ever today. At least since energy consumption of buildings has been restricted, the new types of glass with effective thermal and solar control are key components for creating thermal shells of glass. With the help of computer programs for the realistic simulation of how buildings respond to the climate and knowledge gained from experience with existing buildings, glass facades can be part of an appropriate energy concept. In recent years, new aspects have come to the form in the area of design as well. Dematerialization and transparency are no longer the only objectives that dominate glass architecture. "Materialization" in the form of colored or translucent glass has become a popular means of design, and a variety of products are available.

In all likelihood, such technical innovations as switchable layers, vacuum insulating glass, and self-cleaning surfaces will play more important roles in the future. It is already clear today that the evolution of glass technology is by no means over.

The possibilities of this building material, which continues to open new perspectives on its use and design, makes glass a material with the potential to remain an interesting and exciting field in the future as well.

APPENDIX

STANDARDS, GUIDELINES, REGULATIONS

Glass as material

EN 572	Glass in building–Basic soda lime silicate glass products
EN 1051	Glass in building–Glass blocks and glass pavers
EN 1096	Glass in building–Coated glass
EN 1279, parts 1–6	Glass in building–Insulating glass units
EN 1863	Glass in building–Heat strengthened soda lime silicate glass
EN 12150	Glass in building–Thermally toughened soda lime silicate safety glass
EN 14179	Glass in building–Heat soaked thermally toughened soda lime silicate safety glass
EN ISO 12543	Glass in building–Laminated glass and laminated safety glass
ASTM C1048-04	Standard Specification for Heat-Treated Flat Glass–Kind HS, Kind FT Coated and Uncoated Glass
ASTM C1172-03	Standard Specification for Laminated Architectural Flat Glass
ASTM C1376-03	Standard Specification for Pyrolytic and Vacuum Deposition Coating on Flat Glass
ASTM C1464-06	Standard Specification for Bent Glass

Thermal protection

EN 673	Glass in building–Determination of thermal transmittance (U value)

Sun protection

EN 410	Glass in building–Determination of luminous and solar characteristics of glazing
ISO 9050: 2003	Glass in Building–Determination of light transmittance, Solar direct transmittance, total solar energy transmittance, ultraviolet transmittance and related glazing factors

Security

EN 356	Glass in building–Security glazing–Testing and classification of resistance against manual attack
EN 1063	Glass in building–Security glazing–Testing and classification of resistance against bullet attack

Fire protection

EN 357	Glass in building–Fire resistant glazed elements with transparent or translucent glass products–Classification of fire resistance
EN 13501-1	Fire classification of construction products and building elements–Part 1: Classification using data from reaction to fire tests

Statics, stability

EN 13022	Glass in building–Structural sealant glazing
EN 13474	Glass in building–Design of glass panes
ASTM E2358-04	Standard Specification for the Performance of Glass in Permanent Glass Railing Systems, Guards and Balustrades
ANSI Z97.1-2004	Approved American National Standard–Safety Glazing Materials used in Buildings–Safety Performance Specifications and Methods of Tests
EOTA	Guideline for European Technical Approval for Structural Sealant Glazing Systems (SSGS)

LITERATURE

Achilles, Andreas. "Coloured Glass: Manufacture, Processing, Planning." *Detail: Review of Architecture and Construction Detail* 2 (2007): 184–87.

Button, David, and Brian Pye, eds. *Glass in Building*. Oxford 1993.

Compagno, Andrea. *Intelligente Glasfassaden/Intelligent Glass Façades: Material Anwendung Gestaltung/Material, Practice, Design*. 5th ed. Basel: Birkhäuser Verlag, 2002.

Krippner, Roland, and Florian Musso. *Basics Facade Apertures*. Basel: Birkhäuser, 2008.

Kruft, Hanno-Walter. *A History of Architectural Theory: From Vitruvius to the Present*. London: Zwemmer; New York: Princeton Architectural Press, 1994.

Rice, Peter, and Hugh Dutton. *Structural Glass*, London; New York: E & FN Spon, 1995.

Schittich, Christian, ed. *Building Skins*. Munich: Edition Detail; Basel: Birkhäuser, 2006.

Sobek, Werner. "Glass Structures." *The Structural Engineer* 83/7 (April 2005).

Staib, Gerald, Dieter Balkow, Matthias Schuler, and Werner Sobek. *Glass Construction Manual*. Munich: Edition Detail, 2006.

Weller, Bernhard, and Thomas Schadow. "Structural Use of Glass." *Detail: Review of Architecture and Construction* 2 (2007): 188–90.

Wurm, Jan. *Glass Structures: Design and Construction of Self-Supporting Skins*. Basel: Birkhäuser Verlag, 2007.

THE AUTHORS

Andreas Achilles, engineer, was a lecturer at the Institut für Baukonstruktion und Entwerfen at the Universität Stuttgart, and is now a freelance architect and author based in Stuttgart.

Diane Navratil, engineer (architecture and urban planning), works in the urban planning department in Karlsruhe.

Series editor: Bert Bielefeld
Conception: Bert Bielefeld, Annette Gref
Layout and cover design: Muriel Comby
Translation into English: Stephen Mason, Los
Angeles
English copy editing: Monica Buckland

Library of Congress Control Number: 2008934150

Bibliographic information published by the
German National Library
The German National Library lists this publica-
tion in the Deutsche Nationalbibliografie; detailed
bibliographic data are available on the Internet at
http://dnb.d-nb.de.

This book is also available in a German
(ISBN 978-3-7643-8850-8) and a French
(ISBN 978-3-7643-8852-2) language edition.

© 2009 Birkhäuser Verlag AG
Basel · Boston · Berlin
P.O. Box 133, CH-4010 Basel, Switzerland
Part of Springer Science+Business Media

Printed on acid-free paper produced from
chlorine-free pulp. TCF ∞
Printed in Germany

ISBN 978-3-7643-8851-5
9 8 7 6 5 4 3 2 1   www.birkhauser.ch

Also available from Birkhäuser:

Design

Basics Design and Living
Jan Krebs
978-3-7643-7647-5

Basics Design Ideas
Bert Bielefeld, Sebastian El khouli
978-3-7643-8112-7

Basics Design Methods
Kari Jormakka
978-3-7643-8463-0

Basics Materials
M. Hegger, H. Drexler, M. Zeumer
978-3-7643-7685-7

Basics Spatial Design
Ulrich Exner, Dietrich Pressel
978-3-7643-8848-5

Fundamentals of Presentation

Basics Architectural Photography
Michael Heinrich
978-3-7643-8666-5

Basics CAD
Jan Krebs
978-3-7643-8109-7

Basics Modelbuilding
Alexander Schilling
978-3-7643-7649-9

Basics Technical Drawing
Bert Bielefeld, Isabella Skiba
978-3-7643-7644-4

Construction

Basics Facade Apertures
Roland Krippner, Florian Musso
978-3-7643-8466-1

Basics Loadbearing Systems
Alfred Meistermann
978-3-7643-8107-3

Basics Masonry Construction
Nils Kummer
978-3-7643-7645-1

Basics Roof Construction
Tanja Brotrück
978-3-7643-7683-3

Basics Timber Construction
Ludwig Steiger
978-3-7643-8102-8

Building Services / Building Physics

Basics Room Conditioning
Oliver Klein, Jörg Schlenger
978-3-7643-8664-1

Basics Water Cycles
Doris Haas-Arndt
978-3-7643-8854-6

Professional Practice

Basics Construction Scheduling
Bert Bielefeld
978-3-7643-8873-7

Basics Project Planning
Hartmut Klein
978-3-7643-8469-2

Basics Site Management
Lars-Phillip Rusch
978-3-7643-8104-2

Basics Tendering
Tim Brandt, Sebastian Th. Franssen
978-3-7643-8110-3

Urbanism

Basics Urban Building Blocks
Thorsten Bürklin, Michael Peterek
978-3-7643-8460-9

Landscape Architecture

Basics Designing with Plants
Regine Ellen Wöhrle, Hans-Jörg Wöhrle
978-3-7643-8659-7

Basics Designing with Water
Axel Lohrer
978-3-7643-8662-7

BIRKHÄUSER

Available at your bookshop or at www.birkhauser.ch

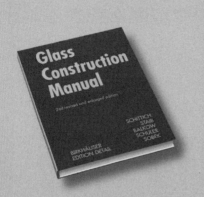